HARRIER

HARRIER
The V/STOL Warrior

John Dibbs with Tony Holmes
Foreword by Bill Bedford

OSPREY
AEROSPACE

Acknowledgements

Although only three names appear on the cover of this volume, a cast of thousands have helped out during its long gestation period. Unfortunately, there are not enough pages in this book for everybody to be personally thanked, but if you feel you should have 'cracked a mention' in this entry and haven't, don't write to us! Anyway, here is the role of honour in no particular order; Lt Cdr Peter West, FONAC PRO; Keith Hanman, Fleet PRO; First Officer Tony Sherlock, RFA PRO; Lt Cdr Dick Hawkins and Lt Dave Gossom, No 800 Sqn; Cdr Chris Thomas; Rod Fredericksen, British Aerospace; POs Chris North and Bryan Sharkey; Leading Phot John Garthwaite; Michael Hill and Dale Donovan, Strike Command PRO; Wg Cdr David Haward, Sqn Ldr 'Fin' Finlayson and Flt Lt 'JD' Davies, No 1417 Flt; Flt Lt Mark Aleandri; Flt Lt Andrew Baatz; Wg Cdr Paul Robinson, Flt Lt Nick Gilchrist and Flt Lt Mike Carter, No 233 OCU; Sqn Ldr Mike Harwood, A & AEE; Andy Probyn, Defence Research Agency; Andy Sephton, Rolls-Royce; George Hall; Hans Halberstadt; Duncan Cubitt; Jon Lake; Bob Archer; Bryan Grant, Flight Refuelling; and *Aircraft Illustrated* magazine.

Published in 1992 by Osprey Publishing Limited
59 Grosvenor Street, London W1X 9DA

© John Dibbs and Tony Holmes 1992

ISBN 1 85532218 8

Written and edited by Tony Holmes
Page design by Paul Kime
Printed in Hong Kong

Front cover *Well into the transitional phase between horizontal and vertical flight, 1st Lt Rick 'Lucky' Buckley prepares to descend onto MCAS Yuma's runway after completing a short bombing hop over the ranges in his AV-8C. One of 15 jets flown by VMA-513 'Flying Nightmares' from marine aviation's main facility in Arizona, this weary 'V/STOL warrior' now resides in the vast desert boneyard at Davis-Monthan AFB (George Hall)*

Back cover *Having just completed the first recovery of a Sea Harrier FRS.Mk 2 aboard an aircraft carrier, British Aerospace test pilot Rod Fredericksen is marshalled away from the stern of HMS Ark Royal (R07), thus giving his wingman, Lt Cdr Simon Hargreaves, room to land on in the second Mk 2. This historic double recovery took place off Land's End on the morning of 6 November 1990, and signalled the commencement of 12 days of solid trials work for both aircraft*

Title page *The best of British! This impressive line-up of representative types based at Royal Naval Air Station Yeovilton was photographed in June 1991 prior to performing a stunning flypast for Her Majesty The Queen, who had flown down to the base to present the Fleet Air Arm with new colours. Heading the 'stack' are six gleaming Sea Harriers FRS.Mk 1s from No 800 Sqn, each aircraft carrying a single dummy AIM-9L Sidewinder missile on the outer wing pylons. Strapped into SHAR '122' was the then squadron boss, Lt Cdr Dick Hawkins, who suffered the misfortune of a split outrigger hydraulic line as he taxied out in his jet, leaving him firmly stuck on the ground*

For a catalogue of all books published by Osprey Aerospace
please write to:

**The Marketing Department, Octopus Illustrated Books,
1st Floor, Michelin House, 81 Fulham Road, London SW3 6RB**

About the authors

John Dibbs has been interested in all things aviation since he was a little lad, being weaned on a diet of Airfix kits and plastic cement in his formative years up in the attic of the family home in north west London. Discovering photography in his teens, John discarded the plastic air force for camera bodies and an assortment of lenses, sharpening his technique during summer holidays spent in Wales near RAF Brawdy. Trained in a central London photographic and design studio, John began working as a freelance aviation photographer three years ago, forging strong links with the burgeoning warbird fraternity of Duxford and North Weald. Now regularly spotted hanging by his lap straps in the back seat of an inverted Harvard, John works as chief photographer for *Warbirds Worldwide* magazine, and is closely affiliated with several historical aircraft organizations in Essex and Cambridgeshire. This is his first book for Osprey Aerospace.

Tony Holmes, originally from Perth, Western Australia, has lived and worked in London for four years. Trained as a photo/journalist at the Curtin University of Technology, Tony has covered the operations of many air forces across the globe, as well as working extensively with the US Navy in the Pacific. Employed full time as technical editor for Osprey Aerospace, Tony has written seven books for this highly respected publishing house including *F-4 Phantom II*, *F-14 Tomcat*, *Seventh Fleet Supercarriers* and *Superbase 8 Fallon*. He is also a regular contributor to several aviation periodicals both in Britain and Australia.

Photo notes

John Dibbs used a mix of Canon EOS 1, 10 and Nikon F4 bodies, mounted with dedicated lenses ranging in size from 28 to 300 mm. Tony Holmes used Nikon F4 and 801 bodies again fitted with similar size lenses. Both photographers used Fuji RDP 100 and Kodachrome 64 film throughout.

Sitting in the hot seat, John Dibbs prepares for the ride of a life-time in a No 233 OCU Harrier T.Mk 4

Re-acquainting himself with the Yeovilton flightline, Tony Holmes stands proudly in front of the FRADU Hunter T.Mk 7 that he has just flown in; rest assured he had a haircut soon after this sortie

Foreword

Man has strived for four decades to combine the versatility of the helicopter with the performance of a high speed combat aircraft. We have seen a multitude of research projects of every type and size incorporating ingenious theoretical innovations. These include the flying bedstead, tail sitting jet and propeller adventures, tilt wings, tilt engines, fans in wings, augmented lift and the uneasy and complex mix of a battery of lift engines and a separate propulsive engine, involving *NINE* power units in all. These are but a few examples.

The only really practical solution to win its operational spurs is the Hawker (now British Aerospace) Harrier with the Bristol Aero Engine (now Rolls-Royce) simple vectored-thrust concept of the Pegasus engine.

Thanks to the small but outstanding teams under Hawker's famous fighter designer Sir Sydney Camm and Bristol's charismatic Technical Director Sir Stanley Hooker, the P.1127, forerunner of the Harrier, first lifted off on 21 October 1960, only 17 months after cutting the first piece of metal.

Significant credit is also due to the American Mutual Weapons Development Program (MWDP), which funded two-thirds of the engine development, with Bristol covering the balance. Hawker boldly funded the airframe initially as a private venture, pending a Ministry of Aviation contract covering two prototypes and four more development aircraft. Without the MWDP's enthusiasm and support there would be no Pegasus engine, and hence no Harrier. Their influence led to a powerful UK partnership with the USA, the USMC, NASA and McDonnell Douglas, which has developed since the first sparkle in the designer's eye some 35 years ago.

The Harrier development is still going strong with major improvements in manoeuvrability, warload/radius of action, and handling and nav/attack systems, all of which enable it to hold its own in many spheres with conventional aircraft, yet enjoy the bonus of V/STOL. In parallel the Pegasus 11–61 engine now generates 23,800 lbs of static thrust, with still further development potential.

The Sea Harrier FRS. Mk 2 is tailored to the Royal Navy's requirements, and incorporates an all weather lookdown/shootdown capability and the beyond visual range missile, AMRAAM.

The Harrier II and Harrier II Plus are joint McDonnell Douglas and British Aerospace programmes providing aircraft for the RAF, USMC, Spanish and Italian Navies, plus future export orders.

Despite all these dramatic improvements, the fundamental concept remains unchanged and retains its basic simplicity. Attitude is controlled on the stick, heading on the rudder, height on the throttle, with but one extra control in the cockpit, *the nozzle selector lever*. This lever controls the thrust vector to meet the demands of V/STOL, hovering and thrust vectoring in forward flight (VIFFING) for air combat.

The Harriers of the Royal Navy and Royal Air Force flew with distinction in the Falklands conflict in 1982 on air combat and ground attack missions. Twenty eight enemy aircraft destroyed without the loss of a Harrier in air combat is no mean achievement. In like vein, in 1991 86 USMC AV-8Bs gave a good account of themselves in the Gulf as part of *Operation Desert Storm*, flying up to 200 sorties per day. The AV-8B also supported the evacuation of US civilians from Liberia in the summer of 1990, and a small force of Harrier GR. Mk 3s remain in Belize as a deterrent to Guatemalan aspirations.

These experiences confirm that V/STOL or S/TOVL as a flexibly based multi-role weapon system, integrated with conventional air power, offers defence chiefs maximum options with which to counter the multi-polar threat environment of the future.

Harrier – the V/STOL Warrior is beautifully presented with excellent photographs and captions covering the latest operational versions of this unique aircraft. It gives the reader an insight into the activities of all the current operators of the Harrier in its many guises, and will provide an enjoyable, yet valuable addition to aeronautical libraries and to book collections of aviation enthusiasts. The author has not spared the rod where in-service development problems are concerned. These, therefore, should be seen as typical of any new aircraft entering service and most have, or are being progressively cured. Evidence of this is the US Marine Corps' brilliant performance in the Gulf.

The Harrier is engraved on my heart and I'm sure this will engrave it on yours as a fitting tribute to 35 years of V/STOL progress.

A W (Bill) Bedford OBE AFC FRAeS
Hawker Experimental Test Pilot then Chief Test Pilot
1951–1967. (Carried out first flights on P.1127 Kestrel and Harrier).

6th March 1992

Contents

The legendary Bill Bedford relaxing in the familiar surroundings of a production Harrier GR.Mk 1 at Dunsfold Airfield

'Flying Leathernecks'

First in, last out! Rather appropriately, Yuma-based VMA-513 'Flying Nightmares' were the last of the original four AV-8A/C frontline squadrons to retire their Harriers to the Aircraft Maintenance and Regeneration Center (AMARC) at Davis-Monthan AFB in Arizona, the unit 'depositing' a total of 16 aircraft just down the road at Tucson between October 1986 and February 1987. Still two years away from its retirement when photographed in June 1985, this early-production AV-8C is seen cruising out towards the nearby weapons range, toting a single 500 lb Mk 82 Snakeye bomb (fuzed with an M904 device) on each of the four underwing hardpoints. The close proximity of the air station to the extensive live range facilities within the county borders has always been appreciated by the squadrons within MAG-13, the pilots of VMA-513 being particularly grateful in the AV-8A/C days because of the aircraft's limited internal fuel capacity! (George Hall)

17 January 1991

As the sun steadily rose in the east, and the desert floor began to warm up after another cool night, all hell broke loose in the empty streets of the border town of Khafji. Several miles away in occupied Kuwait, an Iraqi artillery battery way responding to the Coalition forces' night raids on Baghdad with a steady barrage of 122 mm shells. As the light improved so did the accuracy of the fire, rounds impacting within a nearby oil refinery and peppering US Marine Corps mobile units dug in along the border.

Even before the opening barrage had fallen on Khafji the Marines had radioed for air support to neutralize the artillery threat. The first aircraft on the scene was a veteran Rockwell OV-10A Bronco from VMO-1, the pilot of the twin-turboprop forward air control (FAC) machine circling the artillery at a height of 5000 ft. Taking stock of the situation in a matter of minutes, both the pilot and his observer confirmed the exact grid references of the Iraqi battery in preparation for a relatiatory air strike. Tuned in to the Bronco's radio frequency, and en route to the war zone already, was a four-ship of AV-8B Harrier IIs from VMA-311 'Tomcats', these aircraft having been on alert status from the moment of the first frantic radio call from Khafji.

Based at King Abdul Aziz airfield (a mere 100 miles from the Kuwaiti border) in Saudi Arabia, these aircraft were each armed with four Mk 83 Low-Drag, General Purpose (LDGP) bombs on the inner pylons, a single AIM-9M Sidewinder air-to-air missile on an outer pylon and a General Electric GAU-12A 'Equalizer' five-barrel 25 mm gatling gun housed in an underfuselage pod. Cruising at 20,000 ft, the four-ship rapidly

closed on the Bronco, which had moved out over the Gulf to allow the AV-8Bs an unobstructed run in at the target.

Oblivious to the impending strike, the Iraqi gunners feverishly maintained a steady barrage of fire, their spotters, well dug-in several miles forward of the guns, correcting their fall of shot with every salvo. As the AV-8Bs closed on Khafji each pilot checked that his ordnance was 'live' and that the Hughes AN/ASB-19 ARBS (Angle Rate Bombing System) buried in the extreme nose of the aircraft was operating correctly. The symbology on the head-up display (HUD) confirmed that the aircrafts' Litton AN/ASN-130 INS (Inertial Navigation System) was guiding the formation on exactly the right course, and that the battlefield was only a matter of minutes away. Smoke could be seen on the horizon at an 11 o'clock position and the lead AV-8B pilot commenced a shallow descent to 15,000 ft.

The FAC, meanwhile, had worked out a suitable attack profile that would allow the AV-8Bs to hit the target from behind and pull out after weapons release in the direction of friendly territory, thus minimizing the chances of a damaged jet failing to reach safety. This information was curtly passed on to the pilots, who confirmed that they had visually sighted the OV-10 and were commencing their attack run. Soon after confirming the Bronco's position just off the coast, the pilots got a firm visual on the artillery pieces, muzzle flashes briefly colouring the bleached desert floor below.

Splitting into pairs, they then rolled the AV-8Bs in on the target, maintaining a five-second separation between each jet. Attacking from different directions, and at nose down attitude of 45 degrees, the pilots aimed for an indicated airspeed of 525 knots during the descent. Intelligence reports had stated that most Iraqi units had been equipped with the shoulder-launched SAM-7 *Strella* ground-to-air missile, so the pilots each dispensed chaff from their respective underfuselage launchers during the dive onto the target, as well as dropping high-intensity flares during the egress. Locked on to the cluster of camouflaged artillery pieces, the ARBS calculated the exact time for weapons release, the first pilot guiding a small cross on his HUD, generated by the CCIP (Constantly Computed Impact Point), over a still firing 122 mm gun. As he passed through 6000 ft the bombs were 'pickled' and the pilot immediately pulled back on the control column, his 'speed jeans' inflating rapidly to negate the effect of the five-G currently travelling through his body as a result of this evasive manoeuvre. Jinking away in the direction of Saudi Arabia, and leaving a plume of brightly burning flares in their wake, the AV-8Bs did not hang around to admire the destruction wrought upon the Iraqi emplacement.

Climbing back up to 15,000 ft, the Harrier II pilots maintained a combat spread (1.5 miles separation) back to base. Watching the attacks through binoculars and telescopes, the Marines on the ground and the FAC Bronco crew confirmed that the bombs had been dropped inside the gun revetments and they had then watched the 122 mm weapons topple end over end out across the desert floor; All six Iraqi field pieces had been successfully destroyed.

Thus the saga of the AV-8 in US Marine Corps service entered a new phase on that January morning in 1991. Never before had an American Harrier gone to war, the aircraft having seen almost two decades of peaceful service with the 'Corps up until the Gulf conflict. However, things rapidly charged over the ensuing 41 days of the *Desert Storm* campaign, the 88 AV-8Bs in-theatre flying no less than 3380 sorties and dropping 5.95 million pounds of ordnance on the enemy.

Most sorties flown in the early model Harrier would invariably be less than an hour long, the crews tending to fly more 'cycles' in a day than their ramp mates in Skyhawks and Phantom IIs to compensate for their aircraft's modest range. Returning from a FAC training mission, 1st Lt Rick 'Lucky' Buckley practices a vertical landing in his own 'personalized' AV-8C. The Alpha and Charlie model Harriers were reported to be easier to 'stick' on the ramp than the later Bravos because the exhaust gases circulating beneath the older jets tended to suck the aircraft down during the last 20 ft of the hover. The underfuselage area on the AV-8B, by comparison, has been specially designed to eradicate this 'sticking' problem through the use of two large longitudinal ventral stakes joined at the front by a retractable dam, which improves the overall recirculation of exhaust gases whilst the aircraft is in the hover near to the ground. To successfully land in an AV-8B the pilot must learn when to cut the power, thus reducing the exhaust 'buffer' and allowing the Harrier II to gently touch down (George Hall)

Historically Speaking

Although the 'star and bar' clad AV-8 was new to the theatre of war, and the Harrier II had only been in frontline service with the 'Corps since January 1985, four of the five squadrons which saw combat in the Gulf had operated the V/STOL jet in its earlier form since the early 1970s. It was this wealth of experience on the type that allowed the forward deployed units to maintain an 85 per cent aircraft availability rate across the 60-plus fleet of jets based at the austere King Abdul Aziz airfield, and enabled VMA-331 'Bumblebees' to sustain an average of 72 sorties a day from the deck of the assault carrier US *Nassau* (LHA-4) from 25 February to the end of the war.

Turning the clock back nearly 33 years from the *Desert Storm* campaign to March 1959, the whole V/STOL combat aircraft concept was still very much in its infancy with metal having only just been cut by Hawkers at its Kingston-upon-Thames plant for the first two prototype P.1127s. Six months later the first bench tests of the aircraft's purpose-built powerplant, the then BE.53 Pegasus 1, took placed at Patchway in Bristol. Significantly, although this historic powerplant was designed and tested by Bristol Siddeley Engines Ltd, three-quarters of the minimal monies made available for the

Above *A quick glance into the cockpit of the Harrier revealed an environment not unlike most other fast jets of the same era, although granted the AV-8A 'front office' was a little cramped for a burly Marine. This was no ordinary cockpit however, as a closer inspection of the port console, more specifically the throttle box, showed. The traditional throttle lever had been joined by an extra one which controlled the four nozzles, the pilot being taught the use of this device very early on in ground school! This layout has persisted on the Harrier family of aircraft since the very first P.1127, and many designers and pilots alike believe that this particular arrangement was the key piece of engineering that allowed vectored thrust to be successfully harnessed. In this close-up view, the gloved hand of a 'Corps pilot is gripping the throttle, which he has pushed fully forward. Just below his thumb is the nozzle control lever, whilst between these two devices, locked back towards the striped ejection handle, is the STO (Short Take-Off) stop. This apparatus can be pre-set before take-off by the pilot in any of the incrementally numbered slots along the stop's track – these numbers represent nozzle angle. The switch on the left at the top of the throttle is the speed brake activation button* (George Hall)

Right *This bucket-like device (mounted to an early production model AV-8B) is what the nozzle controller manipulates. The two forward nozzles exhaust roughly 60 per cent of the thrust developed by the Pegasus turbofan engine, and are technically known as the 'cold nozzles' because of the modest 110 degree C-temperature of the airflow as it passes out of the aircraft. The 'cooking' jets at the rear exhaust airflow that has been forced through the combustion chamber of the engine, thus heating it up to a blistering 670 degrees C* (George Hall)

DEFUEL KEY

Above *Some people just can't knock off at 5:00 pm and leave their work behind! The state of North Carolina has long been associated with flying, the Wright Brothers 'slipping the surly bonds' at Kitty Hawk in 1903* (George Hall)

Left *Back on terra firma, 1st Lt Buckley performs the ritual 'ramp dogfight'. Although the Marines bought the Harrier primarily as a close air support jet, they also wrote much of the syllabus on how to 'fight' the aircraft in air-to-air combat as well. Early on in the AV-8A days, a Lt Col Harry Blot performed development work on the VIFF (thrust vectoring in forward flight) technique, which basically saw the pilot manipulating the nozzle lever in such a way that the direction of the Harrier's thrust was altered, resulting in an abrupt nose up pitch combined with a most powerful deceleration. Thus the hunted Harrier became the Harrier hunter! No stresses on the aircraft were revealed during these tests, although Lt Col Blot recommended that the pilot must be well-strapped in before such a manoeuvre was attempted! VIFF-related air combat manoeuvring (ACM) techniques were honed at squadron level by VMA-542 'Flying Tigers' in the mid to late 1970s whilst the unit maintained a six-aircraft detachment at Kadena AFB, on the Japanese island of Okinawa. Assigned to MAG-12 during their time in the Pacific, the squadron regularly participated in ACM sorties with the F-15As of the 18th Tactical Fighter Wing, who were permanently based on the island. After many missions, the USAF pilots believed that the AV-8A was the only aircraft in-theatre that could consistently out manoeuvre the Eagle in a head-to-head dogfight* (George Hall)

Liberally daubed in Spraylat (protective laytex), this weary warrior was one of 18 ex-VMA-542 AV-8s despatched from Cherry Point to Arizona between March and May 1986. In total, 12 AV-8As, 26 AV-8Cs and five TAV-8As are cocooned at the AMARC facility, and considering their age and relative complexity, it seems highly unlikely that any of these aircraft will end up airworthy again. When originally delivered in the early 1970s, this Harrier differed from its equivalent number in the RAF in several key ways. The most obvious external difference was the large dorsal blade aerial which was a vital part of the Sylvania Tactical VHF (Very High Frequency) radio equipment. Other devices fitted included a Magnavox UHF (Ultra High Frequency) and UHF homing system, a radio altimeter and a US-compatible IFF (Identification Friend or Foe) transponder. Initially, the nav/attack system fitted to the AV-8A was identical to that found on the Harrier GR.Mk 1. However, the Marines felt that the Ferranti FE541 inertial nav/attack system was overly sophisticated for their requirements, and presented excessive maintenance problems as a result. Therefore, from the 60th aircraft onwards, this system was replaced by the more austere Smiths I/WAC (Interface/Weapon Aiming Computer), and a two-gyro attitude and heading reference system. The Martin-Baker Mk 9A ejection seat was also eventually replaced by the US-built Stencil S111S-3 system. Finally, the aircraft was given a far greater self-defence capability when the outer wing pylons were wired up to allow it carry AIM-9 Sidewinder missiles. The only drawback of this modification was that the pylons then had to be retained on the aircraft at all times. Although this particular Harrier started life with the 'Corps as an A-model, it ended its days as an AV-8C, having been modestly upgraded along with 46 other aircraft at the Naval Air Rework Center at Cherry Point. Starting in 1979, the conversion programme was initiated to keep the three frontline units stocked with aircraft until sufficient AV-8Bs had been delivered. This AV-8 would have experienced a complete airframe overhaul that included the fitment of new Lift Improvement Devices (LID) mounted either on the ventral fuselage itself, or, as in this case, on the bottom of the Aden gun pods. These LID's were a spin-off development from the AV-8B programme. Self-protection equipment in the form of an AN/ALE-39 chaff/flare dispenser in the rear fuselage and Litton AN/ALR-45F radar warning receiver (RWR) antennas faired into the wingtips and the tailcone were also added, as was an internal on-board oxygen generating system. Known as OBOGS, this device utilized concentrated gas from the excess engine bleed air, thus creating an endless supply of breathable oxygen. In the early days of the AV-8A, the modest LOX (liquid oxygen) bottle capacity of the Harrier had severely limited the 'Corps in its ability to quickly perform a transpacific deployment to or from the MAG-12 bases at Iwakuni and Okinawa

project by NATO came directly from the Mutual Weapons Development Program, funded by the US. Therefore, although the Harrier is a truly British design it can be clearly seen that the aircraft could have remained stillborn were it not for a vital injection of 'greenbacks'.

With this indirect and unofficial vote of confidence in the V/STOL concept at such an early stage in the Harrier saga, it is perhaps a little surprising that another decade was to pass before the Americans finally committed to buying 110 AV-8As for the Marine Corps. Although not directly involved in the early gestation of the aircraft, the US armed forces nevertheless maintained a watching brief on developments. The first opportunity for US service pilots to familiarize themselves with the new jet occurred in 1964 when the tri-partite Anglo-German-American Kestrel Evaluation Squadron was formed to test the militarized P.1127 derivative.

Based at RAF West Raynham, this unique squadron consisted of four RAF, one USAF, one US Navy, two US Army and two Luftwaffe pilots. Significantly, no Marine Corps air crew were invited to participate. Operating from December 1964 to November 1965, the unit flew 938 missions, accumulating some 600 hours of flying in this time. Following completion of the squadron's tasks, six Kestrels were passed over to the Americans, who shipped them back to the States. Designated the XV-6A, the aircraft flew with the USAF at Edwards AFB and performed carrier trials, amongst other things, with the US Navy. Other than two ex-USAF machines passed onto NASA at Langley, Virginia, upon completion of their military trials in 1966, the remaining Kestrels were grounded, the armed forces satisfied that, although the aircraft had some novel flying characteristics, neither the Air Force or the Navy could find a suitable role for it.

With virtually no possibility of a sale of aircraft to the USA, Hawker Siddeley persisted with developing the low risk, low cost P.1127, which was later designated the Harrier, for RAF service following the cancellation of the supersonic P.1154. Meanwhile, in South-east Asia the Americans were fighting an escalating conflict in Vietnam, and the procurement of new weapons to revolutionize the battlefield was viewed as a major priority by defence officials in Washington. By a stroke of luck, a short Harrier marketing film screened for an attentive Maj Gen Keith McCutheon, USMC Deputy Chief of Staff (Air), resulted in two experienced Marine pilots in the form of Col Tom Miller and Lt Col Bud Baker being despatched to the 1968 Farnborough Airshow with explicit orders to carry out a preliminary evaluation on the aircraft. Over three weeks in September the pilots examined the Harrier thoroughly, paying particular attention to its suitability for close air support missions – this task has always been the 'Flying Leatherneck's' prime objective, supporting his buddies on the ground as they perform an amphibious assault on occupied territory.

The Harrier's versatility, relative simplicity and excellent flying characteristics impressed the two-man team, who in turn recommended the aircraft to their superiors. A deal was quickly struck and the first USMC aircraft (BuNo 158384, which was also the 62nd production single-seat Harrier) was delivered in January 1971. Initially, a production agreement was signed with McDonnell Douglas for licence-built Harriers to be constructed at St Louis. However, due to the American system of fiscal procurement, this deal fell through because there were never sufficient numbers of aircraft on order on a yearly basis to allow a production line to be set up and run economically. All 110 aircraft (102 AV-8As and eight TAV-8As) were built and test flown at Kingston and Dunsfold respectively, then crated up and flown to the USA aboard C-141 Starlifters

Above *The last of the breed to be delivered, and therefore quite rightly the last to be retired, the eight two-seat TAV-8As assigned to VMAT-203 'Hawks' soldiered on until the first of the new breed TAV-8Bs were delivered to Cherry Point in March 1987; the final TAV-8A left for Davis-Monthan in November of that year. Virtually identical to the RAF's Harrier T.Mk 2, the TAV-8As were ordered at the end of the production run because the Marine Corps feared that a post-Vietnam Congress could possibly cut the funding on its more vital single-seat order to make the money available for the 'twin-strikers'. The TAV-8s were delivered in the summer of 1976 and immediately absorbed into the ranks of VMAT-203, the first course passing through the two-seat Harrier in August of that year. Equipped with essentially the same systems as the AV-8A, the two-seater differed only in the fitment of a comprehensive suite of Tactical VHF and UHF radios that could be used by either crewmen. This equipment would allow the TAV-8A to perform as a Tactical Air Commander's aircraft in wartime (George Hall)*

Right *Learning from bitter experience the first time around, the Marines got in early with their TAV-8B order, the first aircraft (BuNo 162747) being the 64th airframe built by McDonnell Douglas. When the first crop of AV-8A pilots were trained in the early 1970s, they initially passed through a syllabus which saw them training on A-4 Skyhawks with VMAT-203, as well as notching up 4.5 hours in CH-46 Sea Knight helicopters in an effort to familiarize them with hovering and vertical take-off and landing techniques. Unfortunately this training proved to be more than a little inadequate and the three frontline units suffered the worst accident rates in the 'Corps for several years. However, the advent of a dedicated two-seat trainer soon smoothed out the bumps and pilot throughput at VMAT-203 increased. As with the Alpha-model two-seater, the TAV-8B is essentially a 'twin-stick' derivative of the Harrier II, the only differences being that the trainer is four feet longer with a taller fin to maintain weathercock stability. As befits its training role, the TAV-8B is only fitted with a pair of hardpoints per wing, these pylons being compatible with the LAU-78 rocket launcher, or an ejector rack fitted with six Mk 76 practice bombs. Alternatively, a pair of 300-US gal external tanks can be slung under the wings. A total of 28 TAV-8Bs were ordered by the 'Corps, all of which are now in service with VMAT-203 at Cherry Point (Hans Halberstadt)*

With a crisp salute, a perfectly serviceable AV-8 is 'signed over' to a budding pilot by a watchful plane captain on the Cherry Point ramp. The letters 'KD' on the Marine's cranial signify his allegiance to VMAT-203, this two-letter code also being worn on all the squadron's Harrier IIs. Just as would-be 'AV-8tors' come to VMAT-203 for 22 weeks of intensive training so too do ground crews, nugget Marines spending roughly the same period of time learning their trade on the squadron's aircraft before being posted across the field, or across the continent, to a frontline unit (George Hall)

from RAF Mildenhall (the first six airframes were flown across in venerable C-133 Cargomasters!).

In service, three frontline squadrons equipped with 20 aircraft each were formed: two at MCAS Cherry Point in North Carolina, and one at MCAS Yuma in Arizona. A fourth unit, VMAT-203 'Hawks', was established at Cherry Point to train former Skyhawk and Phantom II pilots in the art of flying the Harrier. Over the ensuing 16 years the small, but highly motivated, Harrier community performed all manner of tasks with their aircraft ranging from WestPac cruises in the Indian and Pacific Oceans aboard assault carriers, to six-monthly forward deployments to MCAS Iwakuni, Japan. The AV-8s remained essentially as per their delivery spec right up until their retirement in 1986, although 47 surviving A-models were modestly upgraded with the inclusion of subtle aerodynamic and avionics improvements, resulting in these airframes being redesignated AV-8Cs.

Back to the Future
The early links forged by Hawker Siddeley with McDonnell Douglas initially seemed little more than a paper agreement as no American construction of the USMC's AV-8As materialized. However, as part of the deal the St Louis-based company obtained both future manufacturing and marketing rights within the USA, and full collaboration with the British on Harrier developments. Similarly, Rolls-Royce signed an agreement with Pratt & Whitney in 1971 covering the future development of the Pegasus/F402 (US military designation) turbofan engine, plus the licence production rights. The future of the Harrier was virtually assured with these two documents, although the main players in the story would now be the Americans.

McDonnell Douglas were first approached by the US Navy on the Marine Corps' behalf in 1976, the manufacturer's receiving a contract for the prototype development

Caught in a North Carolina rain squall, the pilot eases open the throttle and gently unsticks from the soaking runway. From this angle the large fin-like Lift Improvement Devices (LID) and the retractable ventral dam are all clearly visible. These devices trap a considerable amount of the ground-reflected nozzle exhaust gases and convert them into an invisible 'spring' on which the aircraft can propel itself upward. They also reduce the chances of hot gas recirculating into the engine. These removable LIDs are most often seen fitted to AV-8Bs of VMAT-203, frontline units tending to remove them in favour of the podded GAU-12A cannon and ammunition feeder. This aircraft was amongst the first 12 pilot-production Harrier IIs delivered to VMAT-203 in January 1984, its early AV-8A-like paint scheme having begun to weather quite heavily along the wing leading-edges by the time this photograph was taken in November 1985. The 'Hawks' have a fleet of over 20 single-seat AV-8Bs (most of these were delivered in 1984/85) with which to teach pilots the art of weapons delivery Marine Corps style. The course at Cherry Point lasts 22 weeks and will see a successful pilot graduate with 60 hours of AV-8B stick time in his log book. He will leave the 'Hawks' with a 'combat-capable' rating, which is then upgraded to 'combat-ready' status after the pilot has passed strenuous frontline squadron tests. VMAT-203 Harrier IIs wear white tail codes and modex numbers (George Hall)

of an improved Harrier. The main criterion that the new 'Harrier II' had to meet was that the aircraft must have a significantly longer range, and be able to carry more ordnance over that distance. The company's response to this was the thick-winged AV-8B. The new aircraft was basically designed around the re-configured carbon composite wing, its increased span and overall area allowing six underwing hardpoints, as opposed to four on the AV-8A/C, to be fitted. Its short take-off performance was also drastically improved with the addition of single-slotted flaps and leading edge root extensions. Overall, with roughly the same engine power as the 'Harrier 1', the AV-8B could carry 50 per cent more fuel and 70 per cent more ordnance. Internally, the aircraft was also thoroughly reworked, with new systems allowing the AV-8B to hang an encyclopaedic array of ordnance beneath its huge wings. Equally as important, the Harrier II was fitted with avionics that allowed these weapons to be delivered with pin-point accuracy time after time.

The first flight of the AV-8B took place on 5 November 1981 and, unlike many other modern military aircraft projects of the past decade, testing and pre-production development proceeded smoothly. McDonnell Douglas kept costs within the stipulated budget and delivered its first Harrier II to VMAT-203 at Cherry Point in January 1984; well within the contracted in-service completion date. Initially, former AV-8A/C squadrons like VMAs −331, −231 and −542 on the East Coast, and VMA−513 on the West Coast (if you can call 'desert-locked' MCAS Yuma a coastal base!) received the AV-8B, each unit being issued with 15 aircraft.

After a brief lull in the USMC's re-equipment programme in the late 1980s, the second wave of would-be Harrier II units began to break their 30-year ties with the venerable A-4 Skyhawk and embrace the AV-8B. VMAs −311, −214 and −211 (all part of Marine Air Group (MAG) 13 and all based at Yuma) traded in their weary A-4Ms

Above *Fully encumbered with his own personal 'tools of the trade', a young first lieutenant recently arrived at VMA-513 poses in front of 'his' AV-8B. Aside from the oxygen mask and breathing regulator, the remaining bits and pieces constitute the pilot's survival equipment, all of which are attached to a heavy-duty vest that he wears like a waistcoat. Various devices on the vest are activated depending on whether the pilot comes down over the land or in the sea* (George Hall)

Above left *Proving that a Harrier II can roam basically wherever its pilot feels like, a nondescript AV-8 sits out on the grass at a civil airfield in California. Hailing from VMA-513, this aircraft wears a 'Safety S' beneath the cockpit, denoting that the 'Flying Nightmares' have successfully completed 12 months of operational flying without a single mishap either in the air or on the ground. This particular aircraft seems to be wearing a replacement nose section from another AV-8B as the shade of grey on the radome is darker than that which adorns the rest of the fuselage* (George Hall)

Left *Traditionally, training squadrons in the Navy and Marine Corps have provided the display pilot and aircraft for the summer airshow season which runs from April to October in the US. In 1985, the Harrier II was a new addition to the show circuit, and was therefore much in demand across America. The pilot chosen to display the aircraft that season was veteran 'AV-8tor' Capt Glenn 'Birdman' Pheasant, an 'old boy' from the AV-8A/C days at Cherry Point. From nine to five, five days a week, he could be found at VMAT-203 training pilots in the fine art of flying an AV-8B. Come the weekend, he would be unleashed with one of the squadron's Harrier IIs and despatched to an airshow somewhere on the eastern seaboard to perform his now legendary display routine. Above Capt Pheasant's head can be seen the miniature detonating cord (MDC) which shatters the canopy immediately after the pilot has initiated the ejection sequence, and milli-seconds prior to the seat firing out of the cockpit* (George Hall)

Above left *MCAS Yuma is one of the driest spots in the USA, temperatures easily climbing to 45 degrees C in the summer months. As a result, flying at the air station can usually take place all year round. The drawback of the fine weather is the incredible heat that comes with it. Camouflaged with low-level jungle fighting in mind, the AV-8Bs at Yuma literally bake in their own fluids on the flightline, the bulging canopy in particular trapping the heat within the cockpit and roasting the instruments and multi-function displays. In an effort to keep the pilot's bottom burn-free, the groundcrews have rigged up canvas covers which stretch across the open canopies and shield the UPC/Stencel type-10B ejection seats*

Left *Although less than 12 months old when this photograph was taken in August 1988, 'Flying Nightmare 18' was already beginning to exhibit signs of wear and tear, the paint tending to weather along the fuselage frames and avionics bay access door seals. This area of the Harrier has traditionally suffered due to its close proximity to the aft 'hot' nozzles. Wearing the BuNo 163420 on its fin, this particular AV-8B was the second of 14 Harrier IIs delivered to the 'Corps in 1987; most of the airframes on strength with VMA-513 in 1988 had been built in this batch. The white pylon mounted on the outer weapons station is a Sidewinder missile rail, this device often being used in conjunction with a Cubic Corporation Tactical Air Combat Training System (TACTS) pod*

Above *Squadron armourers love the Harrier II because its large, shoulder-mounted wing allows them to drive their MJ-1 'jammers' right under the weapons' hardpoints with little fuss. This VMA-513 machine is about to be mated with a Mk 82 500 lb 'iron' bomb, prior to flying a strike sortie out over the Yuma ranges. When this photograph was taken in 1988, VMA-211 were still operating the A-4M Skyhawk. Four years later, the 'Wake Island Avengers' are equipped with the latest version of the AV-8B, the night attack Harrier II (George Hall)*

The canvas seat cover has been removed on this AV-8B, allowing the XO of VMA-513 to climb aboard and prepare for take-off. Once firmly strapped in (a complex procedure made less tiresome by an experienced plane captain) the pilot will commence his systems checks using the aircraft's auxiliary power generator to fire up the cockpit multi-function displays. To achieve ignition of the Pegasus Mk 105 turbofan, the pilot uses the aircraft's built-in jet fuel starter (JFS) control, which utilizes hydraulic pressure stored in an accumulator within the engine. The JFS spools up the Pegasus, initiating the fuel control system and ignition sequence automatically. At approximately 50 per cent RPM the JFS cuts out, the engine's full generator takes over and the aircraft's hydraulic system becomes operable, recharging the JFS in the process. This system allows the AV-8B to operate independently of start trolleys and external power generators. With his engine idling smoothly the pilot starts to initialize the Harrier II's brain – the Litton AN/ASN-130 INS. He will also work through the aircraft's built-in test programme, which scours the AV-8B's avionics searching for gremlins, as well as checking the Digital Data Indicator (DDI) to ensure that it is properly interfacing with the wide-angle Smiths HUD. Devoid of ordnance on this sortie (and the in-cockpit checks that go with 'things under wings'), he will then signal that everything is functioning as advertised, release the brakes and taxy out to the runway. Stencilled onto the avionics bay access panel just behind the incidence vane is a very subdued rendition of VMA-513's unit badge, which consists predominantly of a wide-eyed 'hoot owl' ready for action 24-hours a day

Cruising along at height north of MCAS Yuma, the boss of VMA-513 guides his specially marked AV-8B ('00' signifies the CO's mount in many Marine Corps units) in the direction of the live weapons range, his Harrier II bombed up and ready for a spot of close air support work with a platoon of ground-based forward air controllers. Many Desert Storm *sorties were flown with Harrier IIs armed up in a similar configuration to this machine, although the squadrons tended to carry only a single AIM-9M on the outer pylons and usually had the gun pods fitted on the centreline stations. The rounded leading-edge root extensions (LERX), which sit above the intakes immediately forward of the wing root, were retrofitted onto the AV-8B prototype to satisfy the RAF's stringent turn performance requirements, these simple devices greatly enhancing the Harrier II's agility during ACM by improving its rate of turn (George Hall)*

With each aircraft wearing a TACTS pod on the outer wing pylons, a neat four-ship formation from VMA-513 returns to Yuma after a low-level strike mission out over the weapons range. As mentioned earlier, the 'Flying Nightmares' were the first squadron to be issued with the AV-8A, early production aircraft arriving at MCAS Beaufort, in South Carolina, on 15 April 1971. Prior to receiving the Harrier, the squadron had been operating the F-4B Phantom II as VMFA-513, completing a tour of duty in Vietnam in 1970. Commanded by the legendary Lt Col Bud Baker, VMA-513 knuckled down to the task of developing operational doctrines for the use of the Harrier in conjunction with an amphibious assault. The squadron's first deployment took them across the USA to the Naval Weapons Center at NAS China Lake, in California, where the 'Flying Nightmares' expended all manner of ordnance, as well as conducting sea trials aboard the helicopter carrier USS Guadalcanal (LPH-7) and the assault landing ship USS Coronado (LPD-11). Back at Beaufort for most of 1972, the squadron again went to sea, this time aboard the Guadalcanal's sister-ship USS Guam (LPH-9), in the North Atlantic in 1973. Whilst embarked, the squadron flew sorties in weather conditions that had grounded the carrier wing's CH-46 and CH-53 helicopters. The following year VMA-513 introduced the AV-8 to the Far East when six jets temporarily operated with MAG-12 at MCAS Iwakuni, Japan, whilst in 1975 the squadron spent six months in the Mediterranean aboard the Guam. In 1976 VMA-513 (along with the other Harrier units in MAG-32) moved north to MCAS Cherry Point, deploying regularly from here to Iwakuni and Kadena over the next eight years. 1984 saw the squadron pack up and move across the continent to MCAS Yuma, thus becoming the sole AV-8 unit within MAG-13 until ex-Skyhawk squadrons VMAs -311, -214 and -211 stood up with Harrier IIs in 1989/90. The first crew training for VMA-513 pilots on the AV-8B took place with VMAT-203 in January 1987, and the squadron was declared operational on the Harrier II in the spring of 1988 (George Hall)

during 1989 for brand new aircraft, the latter two units being the first in the 'Corps to receive the ultimate AV-8B, the Night Attack Harrier II. Currently the 'Cadillac' of all operational Harriers, the Night Attack version is fitted with a GEC sensors FLIR (Forward-looking Infra-Red) sensor, which is linked to a new wide-angle HUD, digital moving-map system, head-down display and night vision goggles (NVGs) for the pilot. Eventually all 328 Harrier IIs either already delivered or on order for the 'Corps will be upgraded to Night Attack standards.

The next generation AV-8B is currently undergoing flight testing as this book goes to press. The Harrier II Plus is basically a full-spec Night Attack aircraft equipped with a tried and trusted Hughes AN/APG-65 pulse-Doppler radar slotted into the slender nose contours of the AV-8B (so slender in fact that the radar antenna had to be trimmed by two inches, thus reducing its interception range by 10 per cent!). This will allow the Harrier II Plus to carry both air-to-air and air-to-surface missiles that require BVR (beyond visual range) guidance to interception. McDonnell Douglas commenced work on the programme in 1987, and in an effort to spread the costs of the project joined forces with export customers Spain and Italy in 1990. The first aircraft are scheduled for delivery to the USMC in early 1993, McDonnell Douglas having been contracted to build 75 airframes to this 'Plus' standard (all part of the overall order for 328). A further 192 Harriers IIs already in service will be upgraded to this spec, funds permitting.

Easily the largest operator of the Harrier II family, the USMC now has the most combat experience with the type also. Backed by a well equipped and technologically advanced manufacturer in McDonnell Douglas, the links forged between the 'Corps and the AV-8 over the last two decades continue to strengthen with the Night Attack and Harrier II Plus versions now coming on-line. Like the 'Flying Leathernecks' who crew the aircraft, the AV-8B is a tough and durable machine that is set to 'Fly Marines' for several decades to come.

Above *Mission accomplished, the pilot taxies his AV-8B off the runway and is marshalled back into his parking spot on the ramp. Compared to the other Harrier II units involved in the Desert Storm campaign (which deployed in squadron strength), VMA-513 was asked to send only six jets to the region. Embarked aboard the assault carrier USS Tarawa (LHA-1), VMA-513 Detachment B sailed into the Persian Gulf with the rest of the 5th Marine Expeditionary Brigade in October 1990. The remaining 14 aircraft of the unit then moved from Yuma to Iwakuni to replace VMA-231, which had been deployed lock, stock and barrel to Saudi Arabia in December 1990. With the air war progressing well for the Coalition forces, and the date for Desert Sabre approaching, the 'Flying Nightmares' disembarked from the Tarawa and set up camp on the crowded flightline at King Abdul Aziz airfield, ready to join the fray as the allies pushed into Kuwait. Although small in number and new to the war, VMA-513 Det B acquitted itself well over the last fortnight of the campaign, losing no aircraft to enemy fire and flying in excess of 150 sorties* (George Hall)

Right *When an AV-8B goes 'tech', or is due for a minor overhaul (and will therefore not be flown for some time), the groundcrews cover all external orifices to stop moisture and foreign object debris (FOD) from collecting in the aircraft's cracks and crevices. Resembling an overdressed extra from a 'red nose day' charity appeal, the CO's mount from VMA-513 sits quietly on the ramp awaiting its turn to be pushed into the squadron hangar, where rectification work will be carried out. Even though the aircraft isn't slated to fly for some considerable period of time, the groundcrews nevertheless crank open the canopy and pull across the canvas to stop the cockpit from 'exploding' due to the heat. Firmly attached to the upper nose of the AV-8B is the all important yaw vane, this device being clearly visible to the pilot over the cockpit coaming*

The second squadron in MAG-13 to re-equip with the AV-8B was VMA-311 'Tomcats', this veteran Marine Corps unit trading in its weary A-4Ms for brand new Harrier IIs in the spring of 1989. Prior to that the unit had flown various models of the Skyhawk since 1958, its final batch of Mike models being left at MCAS Iwakuni in August 1988 for fellow Yuma residents VMA-214 'Black Sheep' to operate when they deployed to MAG-12 as the 'Tomcats'' replacements. Assigned 21 Harrier IIs, the unit quickly established itself with the new jet – so much so that when Iraqi troops marched into Kuwait just over 12 months later VMA-311, under the command of Lt Col Dick White, was placed on a war footing and despatched to the Gulf on August 18/19 1990. Routing via Cherry Point, the AV-8s were supported in their transatlantic crossing by USAF KC-10 Extenders, a type which VMA-311 had never worked with before! After 11 refuellings (mostly at night) during eight and a half hours of flying over the Atlantic, the squadron set down at the Spanish EAV-8 base at Rota. Overnighting here, the 'Tomcats' pushed on across the Mediterranean the following day before finally arriving at Bahrain International Airport on the evening of 19 August. Three days later they moved to within 100 miles of the Kuwaiti border at King Abdul Aziz airfield, the closest Saudi Arabian base to the frontline. VMA-311 was involved from day one of the campaign and flew hundreds of close-air support sorties over Kuwait, operating from Tanajol FOL (Forward Operating Location) as the war progressed. On 28 January 1991, the 'Tomcats' earned the dubious distinction of being the first Harrier squadron in USMC history to lose an aircraft in action, Capt Michael C Berryman of Cleveland, Oklahoma, being shot down by AAA over Kuwait in AV-8B BuNo 163518 (Modex '02'). Although his aircraft was destroyed, Berryman succeeded in ejecting from the stricken AV-8 and was made a POW. No other Harrier IIs from VMA-311 were lost during the campaign, and with Kuwait liberated, the 'Tomcats' departed for Yuma on 10 April 1991 (Robert L Lawson via George Hall)

Over 100 Marine Corps 'AV-8tors' experienced combat during operations in the Gulf, both the pilots and the aircraft acquitting themselves well in the crucible of war. One such 'Flying Leatherneck' was Capt Mike Bonner of VMA-231 'Aces', who deployed with the squadron from Iwakuni to King Abdul Aziz airfield on 22 December 1990. During the course of the conflict Mike flew over 50 sorties, and was awarded the Distinguished Flying Cross (DFC) for the skill and bravery he consistently displayed over the battlefield. He is seen here in front of his own 'personal' AV-8B, this particular aircraft having participated in 41 missions; the impressive total being marked up in the subtle single bomb tally style adopted by the 'Aces' in-theatre. Aside from the bomb marking, each Harrier II in the unit also wore the patriotic 'Free Kuwait' slogan in Arabic beneath the cockpit sill. A close inspection of the stencilled unit badge reveals the letters A and S worn beneath the smaller spades on the playing card, the large spade combining with them to diagonally form the squadron's nickname (Hans Halberstadt)

As with VMA-513, the 'Aces' tend to mark their aircraft on the forward avionics bay door, this panel usually being removed to the paintshop for detailed stencil work. When the Iraqi army marched over the border into Kuwait in the early hours of the morning on 2 August 1990, VMA-231 were just entering their second month of a regular sixth-monthly tour reinforcing the winged assets of MAG-12 at MCAS Iwakuni. The Squadron watched as fellow Cherry Point-based units were despatched to the Gulf in support of the Coalition forces preparing for Operation Desert Storm. By early November the 'Aces' were resigned to the fact that they would have their period on detachment extended to cover for their slated replacements, who by this time were based only 100 miles from the Kuwaiti border. However, President Bush had other ideas and the squadron was called up for duty as part of the second wave of Marine Corps aviation assets despatched to the Gulf. At the end of November VMA-231 was given three weeks notice to get to King Abdul Aziz Airfield, and under the command of Lt Col W R 'Venom' Jones, the 'Aces' duly departed Iwakuni in mid-December, bound initially for Wake Island in the Pacific. From there they island hopped to Hawaii, then, with the help of a KC-10 'mother-ship', the 20 AV-8Bs performed the transpacific leg to Yuma, before then pressing on to Cherry Point. Transiting in the opposite direction was a slightly depleted VMA-513, who had been tasked with taking over VMA-231's MAG-12 commitments until the Gulf crisis had been resolved. After a quick overnight stop at their North Carolina base, the 'Aces' flew the transatlantic crossing to Rota, then completed the final leg of their 18,000-mile odyssey the following day. In just two weeks the squadron had managed to move from one forward deployment to another, all without experiencing any serious logistic or technical problems (Hans Halberstadt)

During Desert Storm, the 'Aces' of VMA-231 were involved in the fighting from day one, initially supporting beleaguered Marines on the Saudi/Kuwaiti border near the town of Khafji. The squadron dropped all manner of munitions on enemy emplacements during the war, the various ordnance used reading like a Janes volume on aerial weaponry; the Mk 7 Cluster Bomb Unit (CBU) configured as a Mk 20 Rockeye II, which consisted of 247 Mk 118 anti-tank bomblets; or as a CBU-59/B anti-Personnel, Anti-Material (APAM) device, equipped with 717 BLU-77/B bomblets; or finally as a CBU-78/B filled with 26 BLU-91/B anti-personnel mines and 38 BLU-92/B Gator anti-tank mines. Four of these CBUs could be carried on the inner pylons. Standard Mk 82 and 83 500 and 1000 lb bombs were also heavily used, the former being configured with either low drag general purpose (LDGP) or Snakeye (SE) high drag fins. Prior to the ground war commencing, AV-8Bs were also tasked with clearing oil-filled Iraqi trenches in Kuwait, the Harrier IIs being equipped with Mk 77 500 lb Napalm cannisters which would ignite and burn off the oil once dropped. CBU-55 and -72 500 lb fuel-air explosives were also employed to clear Iraqi minefields, these weapons essentially consisting of a Suspension Underwing Unit (SUU) -49 disperser coupled with three BLU-73 bomblets. Laser-guided bombs (LGB) in the form of GBU-12D/B 500 lb Paveway II and GBU-16B/B 1000 lb Paveway II devices were also utilized for precision anti-armour strikes, and general purpose 2.75 and 5.0 in folding fin aerial rockets (FFAR) came in handy for knocking out lightly armoured vehicles. A small number of AGM-65E Maverick missiles were also fired by AV-8Bs against armoured targets. As with the other Gulf-deployed units, VMA-231 dispensed with its traditional jungle camouflage scheme before it left Iwakuni. The ghost grey shades were developed from the paint stocks held on the island for fellow MAG-12 F/A-18 units stationed there, the darker shade being achieved with the addition of a 'styrofoam coffee cup full of black paint' added to the stock colour according to Lt Col 'Venom' Jones. The large intakes on the AV-8B were also resprayed gloss white to reduce the shadow created by the inlets from a head on angle. VMA-231 used their traditional 'SHANK' callsign in the Gulf, although the only squadron jet lost in-theatre was operating under the callsign of 'JUMP 57' when it was hit by a SAM over Kuwait on 9 February 1991. Flying AV-8B BuNo 162081 (Modex '09') was Capt Russell A C 'Bart' Sanborn of Deland, Florida, who, having successfully ejected from his stricken aircraft, was made a POW soon after landing on Kuwaiti soil (Hans Halberstadt)

Above *Currently, the most potent Harrier IIs in service are the AV-8B(NA) (Night Attack) variants operated by Yuma-based squadrons VMA-211 'Wake Island Avengers' and VMA-214 'Black Sheep'. Modified both internally and externally to afford the pilot with true 24-hour mission capabilities, the AV-8B(NA) employs state-of-the-art technology in the form of a GEC Sensors FLIR (Forward Looking Infra-red) device scabbed onto the nose of the aircraft which can detect targets on the ground at considerable distances. Coupled with Night Vision Goggle (NVG)-compatible cockpit lighting for use with Catseye NVGs, and two additional multi-purpose colour displays (MPCD) – one Smiths Industries Head Down Display and a Honeywell colour digital moving map, both of which can display TV and FLIR images – the AV-8B(NA) is considerably more effective in precision strikes than its baseline cousin. Additional upward-firing Goodyear/Tractor AN/ALE-39 chaff/flare dispensers have also been faired into the rear fuselage of the AV-8B(NA) just forward of the fin. As can be seen from this head on shot of a brand new 'NA at Cherry Point, McDonnell Douglas has retained the venerable Hughes ASB-19(V)-2 Angle Rate Bombing System (ARBS) in the extreme nose of the aircraft, this device consisting of a combined laser and television camera which computes range and slant angle of the aircraft to the target. Often the laser portion of this highly accurate sensor can be deleted in daylight as the TV camera is powerful enough to track the target on contrast (shadow) lock alone. The boys at St Louis have adopted a smart new overall three-shaded light grey scheme for the new AV-8B(NA) which reputedly gives the aircraft a lower infrared signature (Hans Halberstadt)*

Right *Mounted beneath the fuselage of the AV-8B(NA) immediately below the cockpit is this unusual looking device, reportedly used to break the laser designation of a missile locked on to the Harrier II. Fitted as new on all Night Attack aircraft, this mysterious piece of kit is also appearing retrofitted underneath older AV-8Bs (Hans Halberstadt)*

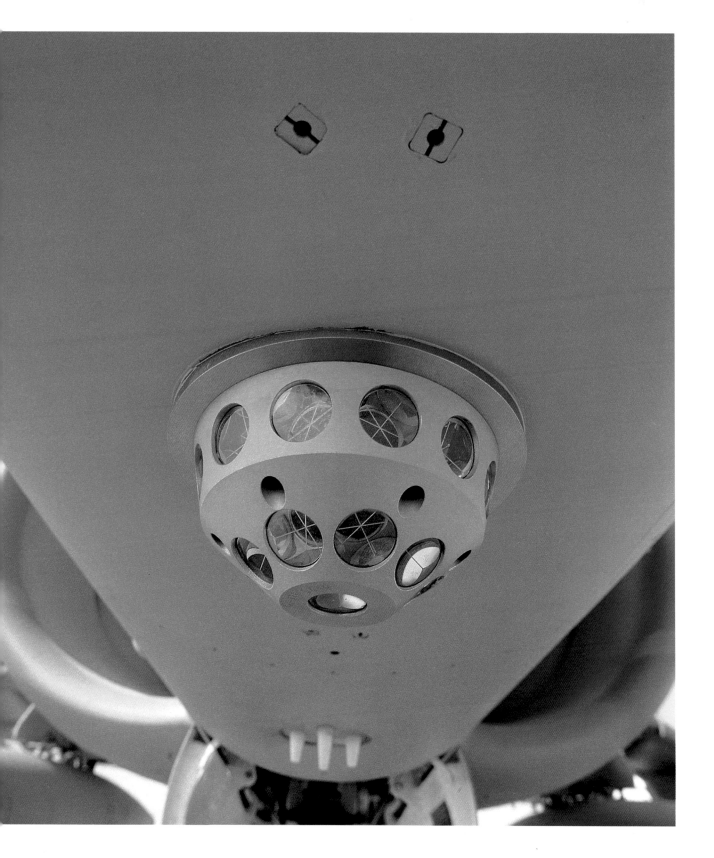

VMA-542 'Flying Tigers', along with VMA-311 'Tomcats', were the first unit to arrive at King Abdul Aziz Airfield on 23 August 1990, the squadron taking up residence in a soccer stadium, and associated parking lot, for the next eight months. Vital fuel was stored in rubber bladders strategically located around the field, and ammunition stacked in shipping containers close to the ramp. Led into battle by Lt Col Ted Herman, the 'Flying Tigers' were assigned all manner of tasks including the destruction of rocket launchers, artillery pieces and Frog missiles, as well as performing armed reconnaissance sorties over 15 by 15 mile sectors of southern Kuwait where the pilots were cleared to hit any 'targets of opportunity'. During the lead up to Desert Sabre, the 'Flying Tigers' switched specifically to anti-armour missions, and on the night of 23 February 1991, the squadron's oldest AV-8B (BuNo 161573) was shot down by a SAM whilst attacking a tank park. The pilot, Capt James 'Trey' Wilbourn, failed to eject and was killed in the resulting crash. This particular airframe was in fact the first of 12 pilot-production aircraft built for the 'Corps, the AV-8B being handed over with due pomp and ceremony to VMAT-203 as the first Harrier II in operational service on 12 January 1984 at Cherry Point. Two days after the death of Capt Wilbourn, fellow 'Flying Tiger' Capt Scott Walsh was also hit by a SAM whilst egressing from his target, although he managed to nurse his mortally wounded Harrier II (BuNo 163190) back to Saudi Arabia before successfully ejecting. One of the few criticisms levelled at the Harrier II after the cessation of hostilities was its general inability to absorb hits from either groundfire or heat-seeking SAMs. Like most other AV-8B operators involved in Desert Storm, VMA-542 resprayed their aircraft immediately prior to deployment, the 'Flying Tigers' taking advantage of this opportunity to re-apply the long absent 'tiger-stripes' to the rudders of their Harrier IIs. This particular marking had not been seen in yellow since the squadron was ordered to change the 'stripes' to black in 1980 (Hans Halberstadt)

Right *Old jet, new paint scheme. Upon the completion of hostilities in the Gulf, VMA-542's remaining 18 airframes were split into groups of 11 and 7 and prepared for the return journey to Cherry Point. The former group, along with all 19 AV-8Bs of VMA-231, flew to Rota where, on 15 March, they were embarked aboard the aircraft carriers USS John F Kennedy (CV-67) and USS Saratoga (CV-60) and despatched back across the Atlantic. The remaining seven jets performed a 'TransLant', with the help of Air Force KC-10s, at the end of March, recovering at Cherry Point on 1 April. Soon after returning to North Carolina, the squadron systematically set about removing the hastily applied, and heavily weathered, ghost greys from their jets, replacing the temporary scheme with the new low IR signature paints applied by McDonnell Douglas to the AV-8B(NA)s. In a somewhat surprising move, the powers that be have let the unit retain their 'tiger stripes' on their resprayed aircraft (Hans Halberstadt)*

Above *To cope with the demands placed on the airflow by the new Pegasus II engine fitted in the AV-8B, the distinctive intake suction relief doors were drastically redesigned. Initially, the number of inlets was decreased from eight (on the AV-8A) to a double row of six, the first 16 AV-8Bs entering 'Corps service with VMAT-203 being configured in this way. However, McDonnell Douglas engineers were not entirely satisfied with this configuration, and after round-the-clock work by a team of 500 specialists at St Louis, the internal layout of the intake was changed and the Harrier II emerged with a single row of larger doors. The change resulted in an increase in engine thrust of at least 600 lbs, improving the aircraft's low-altitude high-speed performance, as well as improving the Harrier II's acceleration. The doors are sucked inward when the pilot slows the aircraft down into the hover, the engine needing to ingest extra air to make up for the lack of forced airflow. Once the pilot transitions back to horizontal flight, the airflow forced through the intakes increases and the extra 'lung capacity' afforded the engine is no longer necessary, the doors automatically closing when the speed change is sensed (Hans Halberstadt)*

The National Aeronautics and Space Administration (NASA) has operated derivatives of the basic P.1127 prototype longer than even the Marine Corps, the organization flying two XV-6A Kestrels from their Langley facility in Virginia from 1966 until the mid-1970s. Currently, the NASA fleet numbers two airframes; N719NA, which is an ex-Marine Corps AV-8A; and the historically significant hybrid N704NA, which served as the first of two prototypes for the Harrier II programme from 1978 until 1984, when it was transferred on permanent loan from the US Department of the Navy and Marine Corps to the NASA-Ames Research Center at NAS Moffett Field, in California. Originally the eleventh AV-8A (BuNo 158394) built at Kingston for the 'Corps, this airframe was given to McDonnell Douglas in the mid-1970s and used for developmental work at St Louis. The aircraft emerged in November 1978 with the new composite wing attached to its otherwise standard fuselage (the twin row blow-in doors had also been fitted), and redesignated a YAV-8B, it took to the skies for the first time on the ninth of that month. Thirteen years later, the pioneering YAV-8B is still regularly flying in support of an international project (which has been running since 1986) researching the all-weather capabilities of V/STOL aircraft. Seen here basking under the blue Californian skies in June 1991, N704NA is being prepared for another sortie at Moffett Field (Hans Halberstadt)

Above *Wearing traditional NASA house colours, N704NA sits quitely in front of the impressive World War 2-vintage hangar that houses the research facility at Moffett Field. Compared to the previous 'at work' photography of the YAV-8B, this specially posed NASA publicity shot shows that the technicians have been busy with the soapy sponges cleaning off the accumulated grime which tends to mark up the elegant white paint scheme immediately aft of the jet nozzles. The fixed instrumentation boom houses sensitive yaw and pitch equipment, and was originally fitted to the airframe by McDonnell Douglas as part of the YAV-8B rebuild. This photo predates the previous images of N704NA (NASA)*

Right *The research at Ames-Dryden has centred primarily around the Harrier's unique V/STOL capabilities, NASA's specialist flight dynamics and flight control engineers checking all phases of the aircraft's launch and recovery routine. The basic aim of the six-year programme is to reduce the pilot's workload in these critical phases through the use of more sophisticated control guidance and command display systems in the cockpit of the aircraft. To help NASA obtain detailed information relating to these areas, computers have been installed in the YAV-8B which are linked to the flight controls. A programmable Head-Up Display has also been fitted. To aid the pilot in launching and landing, an experimental one-levered throttle and nozzle angle device has also been rigged up in the aircraft's cockpit, this revolutionary system allowing the workload experienced during these phases to be appreciably lowered. No longer will the pilot have to take his hand off the throttle during this vital transitionary phase to manipulate the nozzle angle actuator. Other facets of the programme have seen the programmable HUD formatted to display guidance cues for the pilot, the exact mechanical status of his mount, and new symbology instructing him on what flight controls to move next, how much and precisely when (Hans Halberstadt)*

The 'senior' service

As 1992 draws to a close, the small band of nations operating V/STOL jet aircraft welcomes a new member to its ranks. That country is Italy, who, along with Spain, have joined the Americans in developing the radar-equipped Harrier II Plus, the *Aviazone per la Marina* (Italian Navy) having placed an order with St Louis for 16 aircraft. The founding member of this select band of operators is of course Britain, the Royal Air Force having officially formed the Harrier Operational Conversion Team (HCT) at RAF Wittering on 1 April 1969, although the HCT had to wait a further two and a half weeks before its first Harrier GR.Mk 1 (XV746) arrived at the base on 18 April.

Prior to this momentous occasion, the RAF had first committed money to the V/STOL concept in 1963 when contract KC/2Q/016 had been placed with Hawker Siddeley for nine Kestrel F(GA).Mk 1s. Once built, the airframes were issued to the Tripartite Kestrel Evaluation Squadron, who set up shop at RAF West Raynham in October 1964. Rather ironically, the unit shared this quiet Norfolk base with No 1 Sqn, then equipped with Hunter FGA.Mk 9s. This famous outfit later went on to debut the Harrier in RAF service, the 'Fighting First' being declared operational on 1 September 1969.

The ex-Hunter pilots of No 1 Sqn were passed through the HCT at Wittering in six courses between July 1969 and October 1970, the austere training aids of the day (no simulator or, initially, two-seat Harriers) contrasting markedly with the slick set up firmly in place at the base in 1992. The HCT (or Harrier Conversion Unit as it had been retitled on 1 April 1970) was eventually numbered in true Air Force fashion, the unit

The nose contours of the GR.Mk 3 are dominated by the 'Snoopy' fairing which contains both the Ferranti Type 106 laser ranger and marked target seeker (LRMTS), and the F.95 oblique 70 mm reconnaissance camera, the latter's optical panel being clearly visible in this close-up view. The bulge beneath the extreme nose houses an I-band transponder, this device allowing pilots in suitably equipped Harriers to make carrier landing approaches in bad weather. This modification was quickly carried out on 16 GR.Mk 3s chosen by the engineers at RAF Wittering for service in the Falklands with No 1 Sqn aboard the Hermes during Operation Corporate. Other airframes in the RAF's Harrier fleet subsequently received this equipment also. The blade aerial affixed to the transponder is part of the aircraft's IFF (Identification Friend of Foe) suite

Cruising along at altitude, this distinctively marked Harrier belonged to No IV Sqn when it was photographed in January 1991. Now fully equipped with the potent Harrier GR.Mk 7, the squadron transitioned from the venerable Mk 3 to the new night attack aircraft between September 1990 and February 1991. The final GR.Mk 3 mission was flown on 7 December 1990 and most of their aircraft, including this elaborately painted Harrier, were then returned to Wittering. The tail flash was originally applied to the squadron commander's aircraft in celebration of the unit's 75th anniversary. However, several other Harriers also received the garish marking in response to a call from RAFG HQ for squadrons to experiment with making their jets more visible at low-level following a spate of serious mid-air collisions in 1989

becoming No 233 Operational Conversion Unit (OCU) on 1 October 1970. In its former guise, the HCT had only trained pilots who had had previous fast jet experience, the majority of No 1 Sqn's aircrew having many hundreds of Hunter hours in their logbooks. However, with the Wittering-based squadron now up and running, and RAF Germany (RAFG) units (Nos IV and 20 Sqns) rapidly transitioning from Hunters to Harriers, the demand for 'new blood' to feed the ever increasing appetite of the 'Harrier Mafia' resulted in the OCU commencing the first conversion course for *ab initio* pilots fresh from tactical weapons unit training. Started on 1 March 1971, the course lasted three months until 3 May, the students utilizing both GR.Mk 1s and the first two-seat T.Mk 2s to enter service.

As No 233 OCU pressed on with the task of converting both old and new pilots onto the Harrier, No 1 Sqn went about establishing the combat doctrines for the new aircraft, and testing its various systems literally 'out in the field'. Initially, the squadron had experienced problems with the Pegasus powerplant, one pilot having to abort his take-off when the compressor blades of the turbofan separated from the engine and caused a fire. This resulted in the entire Harrier fleet being grounded for the final two months of 1969. However, the New Year saw the unit airborne once again and working furiously to maintain the heavy schedule set for the new type. In March the squadron headed for Cyprus, the nine-ship deployment to Akrotiri marking the aircraft's first overseas trip. Six months later, No 1 Sqn fulfilled their long-standing commitment to the NATO Allied Command Europe (ACE) Mobile Force (Air) when they sent six aircraft to Bardufoss, in Norway, as part of a Northern Area reinforcement exercise. This now annual deployment still continues today.

RAFG

Whilst No 1 Sqn trailblazed across both Britain and Europe in the Harrier, two new units prepared for conversion onto the aircraft. No IV Sqn had a long fighter pedigree

and had been based in Germany for a number of years, whilst No 20 Sqn had been specially recalled from its Singapore home to Wittering prior to being despatched to RAF Wildenrath with Harrier GR.Mk 1s. The transition from Hunters to Harriers progressed smoothly at Wittering, this changeover being aided by ex-No 1 Sqn pilots who were either attached on a permanent basis to one of the new units, or posted to the OCU as instructors, where their recently gained operational experience on the aircraft proved invaluable. No IV Sqn officially 'stood up' at Wildenrath on 1 June 1970, being joined six months later by No 20 Sqn. The final RAFG unit to receive the Harrier was No 3 Sqn, who had previously flown Canberra bombers from Laarbruch. Unlike the other two squadrons, this unit converted straight onto the GR.Mk 1A Harrier (from the second production batch) virtually in situ – No 3 Sqn moved to Wildenrath in January 1972 and worked up on the new aircraft there.

The Mk 1A differed from the standard GR.Mk 1 only in its engine fitment, the former being powered by the uprated Pegasus Mk 102 turbofan which increased the thrust of the powerplant by an extra 1500 lbs to 20,500 lbs, compared to the previous Mk 101 which was capable of 19,000 lbs. This new engine coincided with an order for 17 airframes, which were delivered between June 1971 and January 1972 with the Mk 102 fitted. Eventually most surviving GR.Mk 1s from the first two batches (of 60 and 18 aircraft respectively) were 'up-engined' and redesignated as Mk 1As.

With the RAF now operating at its maximum Harrier strength, the four frontline units formed a significant part of the Air Force's ground attack commitment to NATO. The squadrons honed their off-base deployment skills during special exercises in Germany, and as any everyday matter of course as part of regular TACEVALS (Tactical Evaluation). Close air support (CAS) techniques with ground-based forward air controllers (FAC) were also perfected throughout the 1970s, the pilot's ability to accurately deliver a wide variety of weaponry being greatly boosted when the 'new' GR.Mk 3 Harriers appeared on the scene in 1975. Equipped with a Ferranti Type 106 laser ranger and marked target seeker (LRMTS) in a new nose fairing, which was made compatible with the aircraft's tried and tested FE541 inertial nav/attack system (also built by Ferranti), the reworked Harriers could now deliver laser-guided bombs (LGBs).

Twelve brand new GR.Mk 3s were initially built for the RAF, deliveries taking place between May 1976 and August 1977, whilst another 62 Mk 1/1As were upgraded to this standard. Although the LRMTS was the most obvious distinguishing feature of the GR.Mk 3, the main criterion for the redesignation of the aircraft centred around its new Pegasus engine – the Mk 103 – which developed 21,500 lbs of thrust. Other changes to the aircraft included the fitment of an ARI.18223 passive Radar Warning Receiver, with sensors fitted on the leading edge of the fin and on the tail boom, and a new Lucas 12kVA alternator, plus a Mk 2 gas turbine starter/auxiliary power unit and 6kVA auxiliary generator (both from the same source), which replaced the rather inadequate 4kVA devices previously carried.

Four into three

A reorganization of RAFG Harrier assets in 1977 saw the Wildenrath units moved from their base near Holland to Gutersloh, the Air Force's closest facility to the then East German border. Only two of the three squadrons made the move however, No 20 Sqn being relieved of its GR.Mk 3s and issued with Sepecat Jaguar GR.Mk 1s instead, this transition coinciding with the unit's move to RAF Bruggen. The surplus Harriers were quickly issued to Nos 3 and IV Sqns, who increased their flight strength to three each of

six aircraft. Prior to this, a frontline unit had consisted of 12 aircraft split equally between two flights. No 1 Sqn also increased its overall size in line with the changes experienced in Germany, the unit's brief of rapid deployment within the European theatre being regularly practised both in Norway and in the Mediterranean theatre. Further afield, the squadron was also called upon to defend the former colony of Belize (previously British Honduras) in October 1975 when neighbouring Guatemala threatened to invade. The GR.Mk 1s were chosen for this task because they were the only RAF combat aircraft then in service capable of operating from the short runway at the Belize City Airport. Still in Central America today, a full account on the Harrier GR.Mk 3s of No 1417 Flight appears in the next chapter of this book.

The Harrier's baptism of fire came well into its service career, and rather appropriately it was the vastly experienced No 1 Sqn that 'rode' the aircraft into battle. When the Royal Navy task force was despatched to the South Atlantic in response to the Argentine invasion of the Falkland Islands in April 1982, the squadron was warned that their services may be needed to reinforce the Fleet Air Arm's Sea Harrier units. Sixteen aircraft were selected as candidates for the trip and a combined maintenance force consisting of the unit's regular groundcrew, Wittering's Engineering Wing and British Aerospace civilians worked 24-hour shifts 'navalizing' these GR.Mk 3s. The Harriers were also modified to make them compatible with the AIM-9G Sidewinder, redundant wiring in the wings being utilized to carry signals to the outer wing hardpoints from switchboxes manufactured and installed in the cockpits at Wittering. Improvements to the aircrafts' avionics also allowed the pilots to correctly align their INS systems from a moving ship, thus permitting accurate bomb delivery and navigation. The work up for the pilots with the *Operation Corporate* spec aircraft included ski jump training at Yeovilton, cluster bomb delivery and unguided rocket and Sidewinder firing, as well as rigorous simulated attacks on the Royal Navy's Type 42

Not all ex-No IV Sqn jets found gainful employment after the unit moved on to GR.Mk 7s, this RAFG veteran, for example, being placed in storage at the Air Force's 'hangar boneyard' at St Athan, in Wales. Built as the third airframe in the fourth production batch which consisted of 24 attrition replacements ordered on 16 February 1977, XZ965 entered service with No 3 Sqn in January 1981, coded 'AM'. The aircraft remained with the unit until early 1989 when the first GR.Mk 5s appeared at Gutersloh, XZ965 then being transferred across the flightline to No IV Sqn. Photographed here at Wittering in September 1990, the aircraft is wearing both the old and the new style No IV Sqn badge on the nose and the intake. Not chosen for the Operation Corporate update due to its RAFG ownership, XZ965 has nevertheless received the UHF/VHF 'T-mast' blade aerial mod, as fitted to most Germany-based GR.Mk 3s in the late 1980s

destroyer force; the Argentine Navy operated two vessels of this class.

Eventually, the first three Harriers left RAF St Mawgan for the Ascension Islands, supported by Victor tankers. A total of 14 Harriers saw service in the Falklands conflict flying initially from HMS *Hermes* (R12) and then from a small Forward Operating Base (FOB) known as 'Sid's Strip' at Port San Carlos. Over 150 sorties were flown in a three week period from 20 May to 14 June, targets ranging from artillery pieces to Pucara ground attack aircraft. Cluster Bomb Units, 1000 lb HE bombs and Fleet Air Arm 2-in rocket pods were mostly used, although Paveway laser guided bombs were also dropped; these bolt-on kits consisting of nose and tail fins had been delivered to the task force after they had left the Ascension Islands by Hercules parachute drop.

Of the 14 Harriers despatched to the Falklands three were shot down by triple AAA or SAMs, whilst a fourth experienced a heavy landing at the FOB and was later declared a write-off. No pilots were killed during the conflict, although Flt Lt Jeff Glover was made a POW after he was hit by groundfire over Port Howard on 21 May. No 1 Sqn established a Harrier Detachment (HARDET) at Port Stanley immediately after the cessation of hostilities, this outpost of six GR.Mk 3s eventually being redesignated No 1453 Flight. Tasked specifically with the air-defence role, the Harriers were finally replaced by Phantom FGR.Mk 2s once the new Mount Pleasant airfield was completed on 12 May 1985.

Today, only a handful of GR.Mk 3 Harriers remain in RAF service, the Belize flight being the only frontline element still equipped with the venerable jet. In support of this far flung outpost of the Air Force, the OCU still fly around six GR.Mk 3s at Wittering for back conversion and familiarization training. The two-seat derivative of the GR.Mk 3, the Harrier T.Mk 2/4 is still in widespread use at the base however, and these heavily utilized trainers will probably be the last of the 'Harrier 1' breed retired from service.

Quite possibly the oldest Harrier in operational service when this photograph was taken in September 1990, XV744 had enjoyed a chequered career with the RAF up to this point. Part of the Air Force's initial order for 60 GR.Mk 1s, this aircraft was the seventh Harrier built, and prior to being issued to No 1 Sqn it joined XV741 in the RAF team for the Daily Mail Transatlantic Air Race. The aim of the event was to make the fastest crossing between the city centres of London and New York in either direction. Favourites to set the quickest time were the Fleet Air Arm team equipped with Phantom FG.1s for the ocean leg and Wessexs for the city hops. The Harriers were duly prepared for the flight with 100-gal external tanks, refuelling probes and the rarely used bolt-on ferry wingtips. Unlike the Navy team, who had to land their Phantom FG.1s at a civil airport on the outskirts of both cities and then helicopter the crew into town, the RAF made full use of the Harriers' V/STOL capabilities, launching the race from a disused coal yard at St Pancras and touching down on a wharf on Manhattan Island in a record time of 5 hours and 57 minutes. On the return leg they flew the 3030-mile distance in 5 hours and 31 minutes. Although these times were exceptionally quick, the subsonic Harrier was pipped at the post by the Phantom FG.1/Wessex duo, the last of three Fleet Air Arm runs being performed in a time of 5 hours and 11 minutes, although it should be pointed out that the Navy crews exceeded service restrictions regarding the continuous use of afterburning during the flights. Two decades later, XV744 was still around to celebrate its achievements, the paint shop at the OCU stencilling up the rear fuselage of the aircraft to mark the 20th anniversary in 1989. Having spent virtually all its life at Wittering (first transferred to the OCU in 1972), XV744 was finally retired in early 1991 after the influx of ex-No IV Sqn Harriers allowed the older airframes on the training unit's books to be replaced

SARY TRANS ATLANTIC AIR RACE

Left *The first Harrier hours to appear in any pilots logbook are usually achieved in the front seat of a T.Mk 4 at No 233 OCU, the squadron operating a fleet of 11 or 12 jets in support of its training role. As seems to be standard practice with the RAF, no two-seat Harrier was initially available for pilots converting onto the GR.Mk 1 with No 1 Sqn at Wittering in 1969/70, the prototype T.Mk 2 (XW174) being test flown for the first time on 24 April 1969. Twelve aircraft were initially purchased by the RAF, the majority of these airframes being issued to the OCU. In line with the powerplant changes experienced in the single-seat Harrier, a second version of the twin-sticker, the T.Mk 4, was ordered in the mid-1970s, 14 aircraft in total being built at Kingston with the new Mk 103 Pegasus engine. Eventually, the surviving T.Mk 2s were upgraded to this standard was well. The T.Mk 4 differs from the GR.Mk 3 in several respects other than the obvious tandem cockpit modification. The fuselage is appreciably longer, and to maintain the aircraft's weathercock stability the fin has been increased in height over the standard unit by 18 inches. A larger dorsal strake is also fitted beneath the tail unit. Most T.Mk 4s in service today have a full weapons capability and are kitted out with the LRMTS equipment. In this view the oversize ram air intake bulges for the cockpit pressurization system are clearly visible behind the cranked canopies. Mounted on the front canopy framing is a second yaw vane indicator for the instructor in the rear cockpit*

Above *Defence budgets are continually shrinking and No 233 OCU has had to come up with new training aids to defray the flying costs incurred by the unit each year. One bright spark soon realised that diesel is cheaper per gallon than avtur so the 'Bedford/Harrier GR.Mk 3' training aid was quickly built. The engineering department is still working on its V/STOL capabilities! Seriously, this nose section is used by the RAF's recruitment branch across the country, the ex-front fuselage of XW923 regularly turning up at airshows in the summer months. Originally built as part of the second production batch of 17 GR.Mk 1s, this airframe was initially issued to No 1 Sqn in late 1971. Modified to GR.Mk 3 specs in the mid-1970s, the Harrier was finally written off in a forced landing in Belize whilst in service with No 1417 Flight on 26 May 1981. Flown back to the UK in a Hercules soon after the crash, the forward fuselage section was salvaged and rebuilt. Now possessing the identity of training airframe 8724M, this 'bodyless' GR.Mk 3 must soon be due for retirement*

Jungle warriors

As the sun broke through the hazy cloud, the temperature began to climb. The heat soon raised beads of sweat on the clutch of camouflaged souls sheltering under the khaki netting. This heat was not the gentle warmth of an English summer sun bathing the Otterburn range in Northumberland, or the dry, clean heat that bakes the parched rocks of Cyprus. This heat was the warm, moist type that wrapped you up in an imaginary wet blanket, freshly retrieved from a piping hot bath. This was the heat of Belize, and the heat of New River Lagoon, a most unique training facility for a unique frontline type – the Harrier GR.Mk 3.

Snuggly strapped into his jet, Sqn Ldr John 'Fin' Finlayson guided his mount between the wispy clouds, chasing the distinctive shadow of his Harrier across the mottled savannah. He glanced at the stopwatch firmly fixed to the cockpit coaming at his two o'clock. Almost 10 min to target.

On the ground, PFAC (Primary Forward Air Controller) Flt Lt Andrew Baatz, and his four-man team, had unpacked the 110 lb Bergen, strategically placing the laser designator so that it faced the rusting collection of disembowelled vehicles which made up the Academic Bombing Target on the range. Whilst one man prime the laser, Baatz listened out on his radio for the rapidly closing GR.Mk 3. His headset crackled to life as 'Fin' relayed his position and inquired about any changes to the rear brief that he had been given before departing Belize Airport Camp. 'No changes. Run in from south to north as instructed', was Baatz's reply. 'Roger. Call you leaving,' and the radio went dead.

It might not look like much but this purpose-built concrete pad is home for half of No 1417 Flight's Harrier GR.Mk 3s. Nicknamed 'Charlie Delta' after the single letter codes worn on the fins of the Harriers housed here, this hide is pretty much self-contained, the 12-man team assigned to the GR.Mk 3s living in the camouflaged quarters behind the concrete revetments. 'Charlie Delta', like its sister hide on the other side of the runway, is situated outside the main Airport Camp (APC) complex, and is therefore totally cordoned off by barbed wire. Two of the four revetments are usually occupied by the Harriers, the remaining pair being stocked up with ammunition. A Mercedes Unimog is used to marshal the aircraft about within the hide complex itself. Although conditions may look primitive when compared to Wittering, the geographical location of 'Charlie Delta' does, however, have its advantages; the large complex immediately opposite the hide is the Belikan Brewery, home of Belize's national beer!

'Fin' glanced at his moving map display console in the middle of his instrument panel. He checked that the data begin fed to his Smiths HUD (head-up display) by the Ferranti FE541 Inertial Navigation/Attack System (INAS) correlated with his own mental computations marked out on a well-folded Ordnance Survey map tucked into his kneeboard. With things progressing as they had been briefed, he now commenced the final checks on the ordnance, and activated the Ferranti Type 106 laser ranger and marked target seeker (LRMTS) in the Harrier's nose.

Nestled between the Aden 30 mm cannon pods, four 12.7 kg (28 lb) blue practice bombs sat firmly in their CBLS No 200 carrier, primed and ready for release. Beneath the pitot tube, the metallic 'eyelids' which protect the laser optics from debris damage during take-off peeled back into the nose fairing to expose the shiny glass of the LRMTS.

With only five miles to run and his altitude decreasing, 'Fin' made one last visual check on the 'ballistics box', mounted immediately above the moving map display. Within the box, four slide-in plugs sat in the correct slots, each plug relaying ballistic data about the trajectory of its weapon after release. There was one for the guns, two for the Matra SNEB 68 mm rocket pods, and one for the practice bombs.

Once 'Fin' was satisfied that the plugs were correctly placed, and the appropriate pylon had been selected, he concentrated on aligning the aircraft with his IP (Initial Point). Meanwhile, Baatz had spotted the rapidly closing GR.Mk 3 and given the instruction to 'illuminate' the target with the laser. 'Leaving IP, Charlie, Charlie', the pilot stated. 'Roger', the PFAC replied.

The combined infra-red energy from both lasers clearly picked up the rusty hulks. A small green luminous 'T' appeared on the HUD as 'Fin' peered through his tinted visor at the target ahead. This indicated that the LRMTS had picked up the ground laser cleanly, and was feeding data to the INAS.

'Tango', Baatz heard in his headset. 'Keep the laser steady', he said calmly to the operator. 'Clear', he replied to the pilot. The computer flashed information to 'Fin' on the HUD, and he slightly altered his heading accordingly. The seconds ticked by as he closed on the computed dropping point. Over the target NOW!

Baatz peered through his battered field glasses at the tumbling blue bombs as they left the aircraft and impacted on the target. Two small clods of dry earth shot into the sky as the ordnance ricocheted off of the hulks and buried itself deep in the range.

The Harrier responded immediately as 'Fin' eased the throttle forward and reefed the control column back, his g-suit inflating as it sensed the 6g pull on the airframe. The dry grassland that filled his vision gave way to hazy blue sky as the Harrier accelerated away from New River Lagoon. As the altimeter passed through 400 ft, 'Fin' rolled the aircraft almost inverted and pointed the nose of his GR.Mk 3 back down towards the ground, his air-speed passing through 600 kts as he levelled out barely 100 ft above the jungle canopy. He headed south away from the range for 10 miles before gently turning around in a banking climb to commence his SNEB run.

Airport Camp

Not too long ago, the sight of a Harrier GR.Mk 3 hugging the terrain inbound to the range was virtually an everyday occurrence for the inhabitants of Norfolk, Northumberland and the former border region of East and West Germany, near Gutersloh. Today, the only GR.Mk 3s tasked with frontline duties are the quartet assigned to No 1417 Flight at Belize International Airport.

Split between two autonomous hides ('Foxy Golf' and 'Charlie Delta') situated on either side of the solitary runway, the aircraft are constantly maintained on a 20-min state of readiness by 12-man teams who permanently live within the barbed-wire compounds. This 'on site' arrangement results in the Harriers being serviceable virtually 100 per cent of the time, a figure which is quite remarkable when you consider how old the airframes are, and the distance that spares have to travel when requested. A direct result of this high serviceability is the amount of sorties flown by the four pilots of the flight, each man totalling 28 to 30 hours stick time a month. This continual generation of sorties also has its effect on the aircraft, as Avionics Trade Manager Sgt Greg McIntosh explained. 'If the aircraft sits on the ground for four or five days it is sure to give us problems when we next fire it up. Because of the age of the analogue systems, they tend to jam and seize up if they are not used all the time'.

The maintenance crews and three-man Rectification Team have become adept at improvising 'quick fixes' to the various systems which go unserviceable because of the general dearth of spares. The shortage of parts was particularly acute during the Gulf War, when the weekly Hercules shuttle service was drastically scaled down. Virtually no spares arrived in Belize between November 1990 and March 1991, a huge backlog of parts, including a complete Pegasus Mk 103 engine, eventually being airlifted out to Central America in a chartered Boeing 707–320.

Unfortunately, the conflict in the Middle East was not the only cause of the general shortage of some items. A delay back in the UK on the decision whether to instigate a spares recovery programme on time-expired GR.Mk 3s caused headaches for the groundcrew at No 1417 Flight. 'We are at the end of a very long supply chain when it comes to receiving our bits. With people not so keen on fixing GR. Mk 3s back in the UK now, the third-line maintenance unit that supplies our equipment is busy working on aircraft that have a far higher priority than three or four airframes out here', said Sgt McIntosh.

Perhaps the biggest problem facing the maintenance teams in Belize is the age old Harrier GR.Mk 3 curse – the leaking wing tank. As the seals age with the aircraft, so the weeping become worse. To compound the problem, the split seals cannot be fixed in Belize because the constant humidity affects the PRC bonding material by stopping it from curing. A leak is carried for as long as possible, but eventually the aircraft has to be grounded and the wing shipped back to the UK.

Replacement 'dressed' wings are maintained on standby at Wittering to ensure that an aircraft does not remain grounded for too long. Nevertheless, the maintenance section at the Leicestershire base is finding it increasingly difficult to find spare wings. In 1991 one perfectly serviceable, but wingless, aircraft had to sit in a hangar at Belize Airport for a month while an urgent search of the UK was made for a suitable replacement.

When one Harrier is grounded for a period of time, the knock-on effect on the remaining airframes becomes a problem. 'The aircraft are rotated back to the UK after they have accumulated a certain amount of hours. The problem with this is if we get a bad jet, the good ones tend to be flown more heavily, and therefore run out of hours far earlier, and we end up with a group of unreliable aircraft', explained Sgt Steve Minister, the Flight's Electrical Trade Manager.

Many Harrier GR.Mk 3s have done time in the hides at Belize, but now with operational numbers of this veteran type dwindling, the same airframes are appearing

under the camouflaged netting over and over again. For example, XZ996, which was sent back to St Athan in early 1991 for a minor maintenance period, was sent back to Belize in August to replace XZ998. This continual rotation of a small number of airframes will see No 1417 Flight remain at full strength for at least another year.

The Fab Four

Accompanying the rotation of Harriers through Belize are the few remaining GR.Mk 3 qualified pilots, aircrew being despatched to No 1417 Flight on tours which typically last 18 months. Originally, pilots were sent to the flight on three-month tours, but due to a general shortage of GR.Mk 3 qualified aircrew, the length of the posting was increased drastically. No. 1417 Flight's boss, Wg Cdr David Haward, does not see a dwindling number of qualified pilots causing too many problems in terms of the remaining life of the GR.Mk 3. 'All the pilots going through on the OCU for the GR.Mk 5/7 have all flown the T.4, and the odd trip in a GR.Mk 3, so it is not as much of a back conversion as it would be if they had not operated the T.4', he said.

A lack of currency on type is one problem the flight does not have to worry about at the moment. Between them, the four aircrew have over 5500 hours on the Harrier. Leading by example, Wg Cdr Haward has accumulated over 2200 hours during two tours with RAF Germany, a single stint at No 233 OCU, and his present posting in Belize. Following closely behind is 'Fin' Finlayson, a man who is perhaps more Belizean than British, having completed several tours with the flight prior to his current extended stay of three years! Flt Lt John 'JD' Davies and Ross 'Roscoe' Dawson make up the four, 'JD' being an ex-Vulcan pilot in a 'former life', before seeing the light and joining the Harrier community with No IV Sqn.

Right *Wg Cdr Haward taxies in towards the revetment wall, before steering sharply to his right and applying the brakes once the Harrier is positioned correctly back in its dispersal. This head-on angle reveals many of the lumps and bumps on the elongated nose of the GR.Mk 3. Faired in above the LRMTS's scuffed protective 'eyelids' is the displaced pilot tube, originally fitted in the extreme nose of the GR.Mk 1. The blade aerial forward of the yaw vane is a sensing device for the aircraft's Cossor IFF, whilst the fairing to its left is a ram air intake for the cockpit airconditioning. The prominent bulge at the base of the windscreen is nothing more sinister than a streamlined shroud to protect the windscreen wiper mechanism. Tucked down the side of the instrument panel coaming is the pilot's map of the Belizean coastline*

Left *Although the initial Harrier force in Belize was provided by No 1 Sqn, the permanent GR.Mk 3 detachment set up in 1977 was controlled directly by Strike Command. In 1979 the historically significant No 1417 Flight designation was bestowed upon the Harrier force, and this has remained their title ever since. The Flight is essentially staffed by No 233 OCU personnel, the GR.Mk 3s also hailing from the unit's stocks. Over the past five years the Flight has tended to use a hardcore of six or seven airframes in Belize, these jets being regularly cycled through Wittering and St Athan for minor and major overhauls. This particular aircraft (XZ998) has served exclusively with either the OCU or No 1417 Flight since its acceptance into service in July 1982. First sent to Belize in October 1984, XZ998 is a veteran of over 10 deployments to Central America, and with fellow Flight member XZ971, has provided the Operation Corporate Phase Six AIM-9G Sidewinder capability for the Belize detachment since the mid-1980s*

Safely positioned back in its revetment at 'Foxy Golf' XZ998 is vacated by Wg Cdr Haward, the morning's ACM sortie now over, bar the debrief back in the airconditioned comfort of the No 1417 Flight HQ building (perhaps 'hut' is a better word!), situated within the confines of the APC. The sailfish emblem has been worn on the Belizean Harriers since 1980, and aside from the single letter code on the fin, is the only unit marking to be found on the Flight's aircraft. When No 1 Sqn first deployed with its GR.Mk 1s in 1975, several aircraft were 'customized' in the field with individual tail art, Beech Buggy (XV778), Hot to Trot (XV772) and Rotate One (XV787) all being noted in-theatre. Eighteen months ago the Flight experimented with its own tail art, adorning each airframe with a Ninja Turtle motif. These were quickly removed however, and today the only Ninja Turtles to be found on strength with the Flight reside in 'Charlie Delta's' nature pond!

The CO's foe on this fine July morning was Sqn Ldr John 'Fin' Finlayson in XZ966. No 1417 Flight is the only Harrier unit in the RAF to regularly carry out air interception and air combat manoeuvring sorties, these missions usually consisting of a series of 40-minute two v one flights, performed at medium to high-level out over the coast. Each pilot takes it in turns to be 'bounced' by his fellow Flight members, the defending aircraft relying on the APC-based fighter controllers operating the antiquated SPY-1 'Butcher' radar for precise interception vectoring. Occasionally the pilots also receive guidance from Royal Navy controllers sailing aboard the West Indies Guard Ship when the vessel is in the area. Visible behind the Harrier in this photograph are the rarely worn 300-gal ferry tanks, these bulbous stores only being used in an emergency should the aircraft have to be vacated due to a hurricane alert. On a less dramatic note, the tanks are also dusted off and bolted on when the Flight is asked to send a GR.Mk 3 to a Central or South American airshow. XZ966 was taken on charge in March 1981 and has served with Nos 1 and IV Sqns, as well as with the OCU and No 1417 Flight

The sun doesn't always shine in Belize, especially during the rainy season. Having parked his jet after the brief morning weather flight confirmed the Met Section's, gloomy forecast, 'Fin' Finlayson trudges back to the crew shack at 'Charlie Delta'. The Flight usually performs between six and ten sorties per working day, each trip usually seeing three of the four jets airborne. Missions vary from ACM sorties to live SNEB rocket firing at any one of the three dedicated weapons ranges situated in Belize. Due to the Harrier's traditional short range, each flight rarely last more than an hour, the aircraft quickly being turned around back in the hides ready for the next sortie cycle. Strapped to 'Fin's' flying suit is his Irvin treescape pack, this extremely compact device doubling as a cushion between the pilot's back and the angular shape of the Martin-Baker Mk 9D zero/zero ejection set. 'Fin' is a seasoned veteran of Harrier operations Belizean style, having completed several tours with the flight in the early 1980s, prior to his current extended stay of three years. His mount on this rainy sortie was XZ971, yet another Harrier that has spent its entire operational career with either No 233 OCU or No 1417 Flight since its delivery to the RAF in July 1982

How many tiger tokens do you get for a fully fuelled up Harrier GR.Mk 3?! Even before the pilot has had a chance to fill out his maintenance pro forma, the sweaty groundcrews are swarming all over the jet, rearming and refuelling it in preparation for the next flight. This suitably attired gentleman is not actually restocking the Harrier's internal fuel tanks – he is topping up the demineralized water injection reservoir mounted immediately beneath him. This booster system is vital for operations in the steamy climate of Belize, the demineralized water being introduced to the engine by a turbopump driven by bleed air from the Pegasus powerplant, restoring the thrust output during critical phases in the sortie. The injection system is always used during launches in Belize, the engine's 15-second 'short lift wet' function aiding the Pegasus' tropical performance in trying conditions. The engine is fitted with an electrical jet pipe temperature limiter which restricts the injector's use and stops the powerplant from 'cooking' itself. The limiter cuts the injection once the nozzles are in the rearward position and the undercarriage is up

Although not recommended as a classical 'grade A' posting for career officers, the appeals of Belize for pilots who enjoy their flying, particularly at low-level, are plainly obvious. 'Compared to Europe, we are not penned in all over the place by prohibitive areas. The country is the size of Wales, but only has a population the size of Swansea spread across it. The population numbers about 170,000, of which roughly a third live in Belize City. Therefore, the majority of the country is empty, and we as pilots do not have to worry about major airports, about mink farms or about annoying villagers, because they are just not there. In their place is jungle, mountains, marsh and swamp land. As a result we can get on with our job in a much more open and free fashion than we would be able to in Europe', 'Fin' Finlayson explained.

Only two Notam (Notice to Airmen) areas exist in Belize – one over the local zoo and another over a large cattle ranch to the north of the capital. The mix of unrestricted flying, fine weather and high airframe serviceability usually sees six sorties flown by midday in two waves of three. The remaining aircraft is usually kept ready on the ground in case one of the primary Harriers encounters technical problems prior to launch. The morning push on flying serves the flight well as it means the groundcrews then have all afternoon to rectify any problems encountered during the sorties, allowing them time to declare the Harriers serviceable for the following day.

One other factor also influences the flying programme, as Wg Cdr Haward outlined. 'We have to try and avoid most of the civilian traffic by taking off between 8.30 hrs and 8.45 hrs, and then we have usually recovered before the mid-morning rush. It is a growing concern that the airport's movements are rapidly increasing, as the controllers are inexperienced and largely unqualified in terms of international standards'.

In a typical week's flying, the pilots will fire live ordnance, including SNEB rockets, practice bombs and cannon, on any or all of the three dedicated ranges. New River Lagoon is the closest to Airport Camp (APC) and is therefore used the most, bearing in mind the Harrier's less than generous operational radius. One pilot at a time will usually work the range over, dropping his ordnance and expending rockets and 30 mm shells on separate passes over a period of four to five minutes. Once he has completed his time on task, the pilot will make the short journey back to APC, where upon recovery the Harrier will be rapidly refuelled and re-armed. Whilst the small band of armourers toil away in the humid heat of a Belizean morning, another Harrier will have launched and be working out over the range.

This rapid turnaround of aircraft suits the GR.Mk 3 crews fine, the pilots taking a distinct pride in being basically 'computerless' with their Harriers. 'I think the drawback of many modern aircraft is that you have to sit for hours programming the computers. Our computer is up between our ears, and it is fully programmed when we walk out to the aircraft', retorted 'Fin' Finlayson.

Besides New River Lagoon, ranges at Baldy Beacon and Seven Hills are also utilized, although not as frequently. Baldy Beacon consists of rolling hills and is sometimes socked out with low cloud, thus making it more like a UK facility. It is used primarily as a tactical range for dedicated FAC, whereas New River Lagoon is more academic in nature. Finally, Seven Hills is situated down in the deep south-west of the country, near Rideau Army Camp, and is used infrequently because of the distances involved, and the difficulty in performing accurate FAC from the ground.

The GR.Mk 3 'Fighter'

Unlike any other RAF Harrier unit, No 1417 Flight actively trains its pilots to perform air intercepts and combat manoeuvring on a regular basis. The curriculum usually consists of a series of 40-min two v one sorties out over the coast at medium altitudes. Each pilot takes it in turn to be 'bounced', and the defending Harriers are usually vectored onto the 'aggressor' by fighter controllers operating the ancient SPY-1 'Butcher Radar' back at APC. To add a little variety to this routine, the Harriers regularly work with the Royal Navy's West Indies Guard Ship when the vessel is in the area.

'A lot of mutual incesting goes on between us and them. We attack the ship to exercise their defence systems, and we will also conduct air defence exercises with their embarked fighter controller. They will also tow splash targets for us', said 'Fin' Finlayson.

To add some credibility to the Flight's air defence function, two of the four Harriers have gone through the Operation 'Corporate' Phase Six update, which has seen the aircraft's wiring modified to accept AIM-9G Sidewinders on the outer wing pylons. If a crisis situation arose in the area, further Phase Six airframes held on standby at the Wittering OCU would be rapidly despatched to bolster the Flight's ranks.

The venerable Harrier GR.Mk 3 may have relinquished its V/STOL dominance in the European theatre to its musclebound cousin from Missouri, but in Central America the four veteran jets of No 1417 Flight are still the undisputed 'kings of the jungle'. Only a lack of spare parts and remaining flying hours on the airframes will eventually see the demise of the weary GR.Mk 3 in Belize. However, that is still some time away and there is still a lot of low-level flying to be done. Just ask 'Fin' or 'JD'.

Above *Once as common at RAF bases as the Harrier GR.Mk 3 itself, the French Matra SNEB 155 rocket pod has now all but disappeared from the Air Force's arsenal. Although unguided, the eighteen 68-mm rockets contained in each of these cannisters could still inflict considerable kinetic damage on soft targets, a well-aimed salvo of SNEBs being particularly effective against truck convoys. With an abundance of live SNEBs still available, and No 1417 Flight operating the last Harrier GR.Mk 3s cleared for rocket firing, the four pilots in Belize usually loose off a few rounds over the ranges at least once a week. Here, Sgt Andy Lewis carefully loads each rocket into the pod fresh from the Matra factory crate*

Right *There is a right way and a wrong way to feed 30 mm cannon shells into the Aden gun magazine, and judging by the lack of jams experienced by the Flight in Belize, its groundcrewmen truly are 'Topguns'! This fact is doubly commendable when one considers that there are no dedicated armourers on the Flight's books, each man being essentially a 'jack of all trades'. Each Aden gun pod can hold 150 rounds of ammunition, 100 of these stored in the detachable magazines. The remaining 50 are either in the gun itself or in the ammunition feed chute. Live firing exercises in Belize can be fraught with danger for the Forward Air Controller and his team on the ground as serious scrub fires have been started by rockets, practice bombs and 30 mm shells in the past*

Above *The boss and his jet. Looking a little apprehensive about the interview that was soon to take place with Central Television's Simon Harris, Wg Cdr Haward views proceedings from the cockpit as the reporter, and his cameraman Brian Cave, manoeuvre 'Charlie Delta's' Unimog into position alongside the CO's Harrier prior to commencing filming. David Haward had only recently been promoted to the rank of wing commander when this photograph was taken in July 1991. An experienced pilot with over 2200 Harrier hours in his logbook, Haward had served with both No1 Sqn and No 233 OCU prior to his posting to Belize. Pilots were originally sent to Central America on three-month tours from the European Harrier units, as were the groundcrews. However, with virtually all the GR.Mk 3s now gone, and aircrew experience on the type rapidly disappearing as well, the RAF has changed the flying berths in Belize to voluntary tours of 18 months duration. Currently, there are no plans to swap the Mk 3s for Mk 5s or 7s, the older Harriers calculated to have enough fatigue life left in them for at least another three years*

Right *Once suited up and strapped in the boss looks far more at ease! Framed by his ever faithful groundcrew, Wg Cdr Haward checks his seat and parachute harness before commencing his cockpit checks prior to engine spool up. Due to the limited dimensions of the GR.Mk 3's cockpit, most high time Harrier jocks are of small to medium stature, 'beefy' pilots tending to swap to Tornados or Phantom IIs after a tour or two!*

Troubled cousins

As told in Chapter one of this volume, the Harrier II was successfully blooded in combat over Kuwait by a clutch of Marine Corps units, no less than 88 AV-8Bs dropping an encyclopaedic array of ordnance ranging from napalm cannisters to laser guided bombs. The aircraft's systems stood up to the rigours of war well, and the groundcrews achieved a sustained availability rate of airframes which exceeded 88 per cent. This figure is even more impressive when you consider the austere conditions encountered at King Abdul Aziz airfield, and the continuous sortie rate maintained by the squadrons. Back in the US, the Yuma-based AV-8B(NA) units were also making great progress with their new aircraft, steadily working through the endless operational test programme set out for them prior to receiving the 'ultimate AV-8B'. In short, 1991 was a very good year for the Harrier II in Marine Corps service. Unfortunately, the same could not be said for the Harrier GR.Mk 5/7 community across the Atlantic.

The year started out promisingly enough with No 1 Sqn making the RAF's first Red Flag appearance in the GR.Mk 5 in early March, the unit performing well out over the Nellis ranges in all mission profiles. Back in Europe, No 3 Sqn was nearing its second anniversary on the Harrier II, having received its first aircraft (ZD401) on 17 March 1989. Although still restricted to expending AIM-9 Sidewinders and 3 kg practice bombs, or cluster bomb units, only , the squadron was nevertheless pressing on with its in-theatre exercise programme, regularly deploying aircraft to dispersed sites in the Sennelager area. Across the ramp at Gutersloh, No IV Sqn too was getting to grips with its new mounts, the GR.Mk 7s drastically increasing the squadron's operational capabilities since their introduction to service in September 1990.

Cruising along at height over the wilds of Cambridgeshire, a 'nude' Harrier GR.Mk 5 of No 233 OCU maintains a loose formation with the T.Mk 4 photoship. At the controls of ZD346 is Flt Lt Nick Gilchrist, a highly experienced Harrier operator, and the man chosen as display pilot for the GR.Mk 5's debut season on the summer airshow circuit in 1990. This Harrier is configured in typical OCU guise, the unit's 14 GR.Mk 5s rarely carrying external stores, bar the occasional practice bomb launcher for weapons training. From this angle, the demarcation line between the two shades of green that form the Harrier II's distinctive camouflage scheme is readily apparent, the paler shade (known as Lichen) covering the entire undersurface of the aircraft. This scheme was chosen for the new Harriers after Nos 3 and IV Sqns carried out Operation Match-Coat in 1984. A single GR.Mk 3 from each squadron was painted up in vastly different colours from those traditionally worn by RAFG units; No 3 Sqn's XV804 adopted the olive greens, whilst XV738 was camouflaged in an attractive two-tone grey scheme. Both aircraft used the same demarcation template of the darker shade on top and the lighter colour underneath, with No IV Sqn even going as far as to re-applying the unit's distinctive nose flash in grey!

However, things began to go awry on 29 May at Gutersloh when a No IV Sqn
GR.Mk 7 crashed near the base soon after take-off. Fortunately, the pilot ejected safely
and was able to report that the aircraft had suffered a total electrical failure. Despite a
thorough investigation of the wreckage no fault could be traced and operations were
resumed in early June. Unfortunately two separate incidents in late July placed the
spotlight on the aircraft once again. On 16 July another No IV Sqn jet suffered total
electrical failure and an electrical systems fire, although the pilot managed to return to
base where the fire was quickly extinguished. Less than two weeks later on 29 July a
Wittering-based GR.Mk 5 experienced electrical failure and a severe internal fire in the
rear fuselage equipment bay, the pilot again being able to successfully return to base
and land, although the Harrier II was severely damaged by the conflagration. These
incidents, plus several earlier electrical failures which had left other aircraft with
emergency battery power only, resulted in the grounding of the entire 79-strong
GR.Mk 5/7 fleet at the end of July.

The fires were traced to wiring in the distribution loom of the transformer rectifier
unit, housed in the rear equipment bay. The thin layer of carbon insulation which
protected the wiring was slowly being chaffed away due to the looms contacting each
other, the resulting shorts knocking out the electrics and causing fierce fires. The power
switching panel for the rectifier unit was also found to be faulty, this equipment
operating on a normal sortie at its maximum specification, leaving no room to absorb
periodic power surges. During the seven-week long grounding British Aerospace
engineers worked feverishly to come up with a quick-fix solution to the problem, their
efforts resulting in the power switching panel being fitted with a heavy duty contactor,
and smaller electrical connector tags being fitted to increase the clearance between
looms, plus general reworking of the equipment bay with new lightweight Tefzel
wiring. To allow the squadrons to commence operations as soon as possible, British

Although the OCU received its first GR.Mk 5 on 29 May 1987, a freak accident experienced by a pre-delivery Harrier II in British Aerospace hands in October of that year halted any serious training until July 1988 when the Harrier Conversion Team (HCT) was stood up at Wittering. Charged with the responsibility of training experienced No 1 Sqn pilots in the art of Harrier flying, GR.Mk 5 style, the HCT performed this task both quickly and efficiently, the unit redeclaring itself to NATO on 2 November 1989. With this job over, the HCT was disbanded and the OCU was able to commence its first 'long course' on the aircraft for brand new pilots. Although conversion training is the unit's primary tasking, other duties are also performed. These include schooling for potential Harrier instructors – Qualified Weapons Instructor (QWI) and Qualified Flying Instructor (QFI) courses are regularly run – as well as performing refresher courses for qualified Harrier pilots returning to the V/STOL community after 'desk' tours. To help the unit cope with the different demands placed on its instructors by the mixed bag of novice and experienced pilots, the OCU is split into two flights; 'A' (Advanced) Squadron which handles postgraduate work and weapons instruction for new pilots progressing through the course; and 'B' (Basic) Squadron, which, as it suggests, receives aircrew fresh from a Tactical Weapons Unit or from another fast jet community. Flt Lt Gilchrist enjoys the dual qualification of being both a QFI and a QWI, his vast experience on the Harrier stretching back to the early 1980s with No 1 Sqn over the Falkland Islands. Chosen to fly one of four attrition replacement GR.Mk 3s down to the taskforce, Flt Lt Gilchrist, along with Kiwi squadron mate Flt Lt Russ Boyens, set out from Ascension Island on 8 June 1982 bound for the Hermes, 3900 miles away. Escorted part of the way by a Victor tanker, the pair recovered aboard the carrier after an eight and a half hour flight following the route taken by two other GR.Mk 3s that had preceded them on 1 June. Following a brief acclimatization period aboard ship, Gilchrist was blooded over the Falklands when he accompanied Flt Lt Tony Harper on a CBU strike against a column of troops marching across Sapper Hill on the afternoon of 12 June. Two days later he was airborne again, his Harrier equipped with two Paveway laser guided bombs. Lining up for their attack on an enemy position in the hills above Port Stanley, the pilots were excitedly instructed by the FAC on the ground (who was providing the laser designation for them) that the Argentine forces were flying the white flag and retreating towards the town. Aborting their strike, the pilots returned to the carrier and imparted this historic news to the ship's crew

Aerospace carried out on-site modifications to the aircraft, roughly half of the fleet being airworthy again by late September. Even then pilots were still restricted to flying sorties that saw them no more than 20 minutes flying time away from a suitable landing site. For permanent repairs to be carried out further mass groundings would have to take place so the RAF have decided not to carry out full modifications until the aircraft are due for major overhaul.

More bad news hit the Harrier community in late summer, although in this case it wasn't just restricted to the RAF. Severe acoustic fatigue cracking in the rear fuselage caused by the rear exhaust nozzles had been noticed on USMC AV-8Bs, and when RAF engineers took a closer look at their GR.Mk 5/7s they also noticed the same problem, although to a lesser degree due to the younger age of their aircraft. Reports have suggested that up to 250 Harrier IIs could be affected by this daunting problem, with both McDonnell Douglas and British Aerospace quickly coming up with an interim repair programme that has seen an aluminium patch, and minor structural modifications, built into the airframe; this quick-fix sees the aircraft grounded for three to four weeks. The only way to permanently eradicate the fatigue cracks however, is to rebuild the centre-fuselage, the internal stringers being doubled and reinforcement aluminium skinning from frame 27 through to frame 33 being added. Earlier USMC and RAF Harrier IIs are being repaired as they pass through the Night Attack conversion programme at St Louis and Kingston respectively, the cost of this additional work reportedly being met by the manufacturers.

Enhanced capability

Although the Harrier II episode up to this point has not been an entirely happy one for the RAF, the GR.Mk 5/7 has still drastically upgraded the potency of its small attack community. Based closely on the AV-8B, the anglicized Harrier II differs mainly in detail changes to its avionics suite, threat warning and ECM fitment, and the choice of external cannon. The GR.Mk 7 shares the same FLIR and associated cockpit displays with the AV-8B(NA), although the RAF pilot wears different NVGs. Elsewhere in the cockpit, the latest version of the Ferranti moving map display is also fitted, a similar device only now appearing in the USMC Harrier IIs. The INS in some of the GR.5s is American however, the Litton AN/ASN-130 unit being bought after the Ferranti FIN 1075 failed to initially function with any reliability. This device has now been sorted and is fitted as standard in new-build GR.7s. The communication transceiver is of British design (GEC Avionics ED 3500), as are the IFF transponders (Cossor IFF 4760).

The Marconi ZEUS RWR/ECM suite is more capable than the Litton AN/ALR-67 that it replaces, the system being able to both detect and jam the threat frequency as opposed to just warning the pilot about it. A Plessey Missile Approach Warning (MAW) system developed specifically for the new RAF Harrier fleet is carried in the tailcone of the aircraft, alerting the pilot of missile threats approaching from the rear quarter. On a more offensive note, the Royal Ordnance Faction Aden 25 mm cannon specially built for the GR.Mk 5/7 promises to be a superbly accurate weapon when it finally passes its installation trials. Delayed over two years by fitment problems, the gun is currently expected to enter service in mid-1993.

The Harrier II community has of late experienced more than its fair share of dramas, the aircraft taking longer to reach maturity than perhaps it should have. Although the GR.Mk 5/7 is currently not as capable as its American cousin, the definitive RAF aircraft will eventually possess an ability to get the job done that exceeds the AV-8B(NA). With the ZEUS system fully operable, twin ADEN cannons slung under the fuselage and all nine hard points bombed (and missiled) up, the GR.Mk 7 promises to be a formidable weapon in any future order of battle.

While his mate keeps a watchful eye on proceedings from ramp level, a corporal from No 1 Sqn goes 'head down' into the cockpit of this newly delivered GR.Mk 5. The bulging of the forward fuselage on the later model Harrier is readily apparent from this nose on view, the large mass of the instrument coaming being particularly prominent. Sat on the lip of the coaming is the Smiths Industries wide-angle SU-128/A HUD, this impressive device being mounted immediately above its push button menu – the 'up-front control set' – which allows the pilot to manipulate communications, identification, navigation and weapons selection by operating either the key pad, or the control column thumb switch

Above *Besides the Soviet contingent that appeared in force at the Farnborough display in September 1990, the most impressive performance of the week was the afternoon scramble undertaken with skill and vigour by eight GR.Mk 5s of No 1 Sqn. Celebrating the unit's 70-year association with the famous Hampshire airfield, No 1 Sqn also paid tribute to the pilots of Fighter Command, who had been defending Britain from Luftwaffe attacks exactly 50 years ago that month. The airshow routine consisted of two flights of four jets launching at each other in opposite directions from the grass field in between the main runways. Once the dust had settled, the Harrier pilots then 'strafed' the airfield, before joining up in a line abreast formation and positioning themselves along the crowd line. The famous V/STOL routine then followed, the accompanying sound of eight Pegasus turbofans causing many an instant headache amongst awestruck spectators on the ground. Having completed yet another impressive performance, ZD409 is guided down the runway back to the 'live-side' dispersal hidden behind the fir trees. Seventy years earlier, the squadron had been operating airships under the guise of No 1 Company of the Air Battalion, Royal Engineers; these devices also possessed a V/STOL capability!*

Left *Like the AV-8B, the GR.Mk 5/7 accommodates the Hughes ASB-19(V)2 Angle Rate Bombing System (ARBS) in its extreme nose. Originally built to fulfil a USMC requirement in 1975, the first systems entered service in the Corps' A-4M Skyhawks, the ARBS proving both cheap to maintain and very effective operationally. The V-shaped chin fairing beneath the ARBS is all that remains of a system developed especially for the RAF Harrier IIs which proved to be neither cheap or effective. The MIRLS (Miniature Infra-red Linescan System) was designed to provide the aircraft with a device that recorded data directly onto video tape, this machine, in theory at least, being vastly superior to the venerable oblique F.95 camera fitted in the GR.Mk 3 and used extensively in the vital armed-reconnaissance role. Developed from the system fitted in the Tornado GR.Mk 1A, the MIRLS was eventually cancelled due to developmental problems and cost overruns. Although all the GR.Mk 5s built for the RAF were delivered with the empty bulge beneath the nose, the later Mk 7s have had this fairing deleted (as the Mk 5s are returned to British Aerospace for upgrading to definitive Harrier II specs, the fairings are being removed). This unfortunate situation currently leaves the RAF's Harrier II force totally devoid of any reconnaissance capability, although the Ministry of Defence have been casting an envious eye over podded linescan devices currently in service with the US Navy*

Below *Flt Lt Gilchrist sits in the hover just feet above the lush green countryside that surrounds Wittering. This is as close as you can physically get to the GR.5 in the hover whilst strapped into a T.Mk 4 - any closer and the hot gases expelled from the Harrier could be ingested by the 'twin-sticker', resulting in a rapid loss of power and lift*

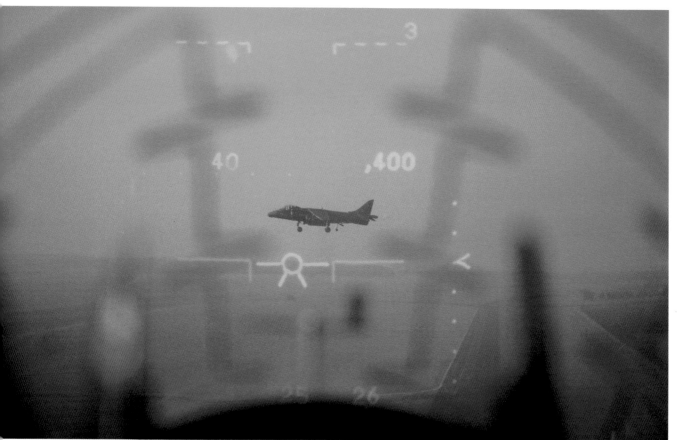

Pulling away from the crowdline having finished his hovering routine, the pilot banks ZD379 around, revealing the aircraft's underside details to the camera. British Aerospace took advantage of the strengthening around the repositioned wing outriggers on the GR.Mk 5/7 to add two extra pylons optimized purely for the AIM-9 Sidewinder missile; this extra pair of hardpoints is currently not available on the AV-8B. Unlike its sister aircraft illustrated on page 74, ZD379 carries a pair of 25 mm dummy Aden cannon pods under the fuselage, as well as a rarely seen centreline pylon between the 'guns'

Above left *September 1990 was a busy month for RAF stations across Britain, the airspace overhead many of these bases playing host to some of the largest formations of Air Force aircraft seen aloft since the Queen's coronation in 1952. These mass sorties served as dress rehearsals for the huge flypast which took place over central London on Battle of Britain day (15 September). A blanket request was sent out to all units asking for their participation in the event, and one of half a dozen squadrons to answer the call from RAFG was No 3 Sqn, who had only re-declared themselves to NATO the previous April following a successful transition from GR.Mk 3 to Mk 5. The final rehearsal flypast completed, a solitary Harrier II from the Gutersloh-based unit slowly approaches the 'piano keys' at the runway threshold having already passed over the A1. The GR.Mk 5/7's huge composite wing has effectively slowed the Harrier II's landing speed (85 knots) by 35 knots when compared to the GR.Mk 3 (120 knots)*

Above right *'Cockatrice tail feathers' ranged up at Wittering. The RAF has traditionally restricted tail markings on its Harriers to the fin flash and the squadrons' individual aircraft identification code; No 3 Sqn, for example, has worn A-prefixed letters since July 1980. With the advent of the GR.Mk 5 however, the squadron decided to liven up the appearance of its Harrier IIs a little by applying unit colours of green and yellow to the extreme fin tips. Although a welcome addition to the aircraft, the fin stripe is perhaps a little overshadowed by the bright formation lighting strip flush to the vertical surface*

The ultimate Harrier II currently in service is the GR.Mk 7, which is used exclusively in a frontline capacity by No IV Sqn. Essentially a GR.Mk 5 with night attack capabilities, the aircraft has been subjected to rigorous testing by both British Aerospace and the Strike/Attack Operational Evaluation Unit (SAOEU) at Boscombe Down prior to its service release. This particular aircraft (ZG472) is one of a pair of Mk 7s currently attached to the SAOEU, the unit continuing to utilize the first two production night attack Harrier IIs delivered to the RAF for trials work connected with both the NVG equipment and the Marconi Zeus ECM suite. Although the Mk 7 has greater offensive capabilities than the Mk 5, it is not a truly all-weather attack aircraft like the Tornado GR.Mk 1 or the A-6E Intruder. The nose mounted FLIR and the pilot's NVGs give the aircraft a handy clear-night capability, although should the weather turn bad the Mk 7's avionics would be hard pressed to find the target. The twin antennae under the ARBS on the Mk 7 are the forward hemisphere receivers for the complex Zeus equipment. This two-tiered system combines Marconi radar warning receivers with an automatically activated, rapid response Northrop jammer, the overall system also being compatible with the aircraft's other self-protection devices. Initially afflicted with some serious reliability problems, the Zeus system was given a thorough overhaul by the manufacturer and then put through its paces by three SAOEU GR.Mk 7s at the US Navy's sophisticated ECM range at China Lake, in California, in the early summer of 1989. After 50 trial sorties and some more minor tweaking by Marconi, the system was finally declared fit for operational service in mid-1990

One of the key items of equipment available to GR.Mk 7 crews are the horrifyingly expensive night vision goggles (NVG) which allow the wearer to 'look into' his next manoeuvre, and bestow upon him some freedom of movement within the cockpit. The image presented through the goggles is not as sharp as that generated by the FLIR, and flashed up on the HUD, but the NVGs are not restricted to the former system's 22-degree field of view. Pilots have found that flying low-level missions with the NVGs is an extremely tiring affair, although the fatigue factor can be lowered significantly with regular use. The SAOEU has been heavily involved in both the testing and operational application of the goggles, its small crop of highly experienced pilots first being introduced to them in a series of check rides in one of the unit's two T.Mk 4s. This particular aircraft (XW269) has seen service with all three frontline units, plus the OCU, at one time or another during its long career. Originally built in 1971 as part of the RAF's first order for a dozen T.Mk 2s, XW269 was despatched from No IV Sqn to the SAOEU in 1989, where it joined sister-aircraft XW267 in the 'Nightbird' GR.Mk 7 avionics and equipment trials

SHAR

Ten years ago a small band of highly motivated individuals were tasked with the responsibility of protecting the largest flotilla of Royal Navy warships assembled since World War 2. Operating thousands of miles from friendly territory in an aircraft that was originally built for the close air support role, these pilots were also aware of the fact that they had to shoot the enemy's fighter and attack aircraft down at a rate of 10 to 1. The resulting combats over the Falkland Islands are now legendary, the Fleet Air Arm's fighter squadrons performing to their fullest capability. Although the majority of the pilots involved in the conflict have now either moved 'upstairs' to staff posting, or left the Navy entirely, their mounts in the South Atlantic still grace the carrier decks, or the ramp at Royal Naval Air Station (RNAS) Yeovilton, today. That aircraft is of course the Sea Harrier FRS.Mk 1.

The first 'navalized' Harrier was delivered to the Fleet Air Arm on 18 June 1979, XZ451 (which was later used to shoot down three Argentine aircraft) going to the recently commissioned No 700A Sqn. In true naval tradition, this special unit had been formed to oversee the FRS.Mk 1's entry into service, the squadron being designated an Intensive Flying Trials Unit (IFTU). Based at Yeovilton, No 700A Sqn took charge of the first five Sea Harriers delivered from Dunsfold and commenced operational trials (which included an embarkation aboard the *Hermes*) that lasted until the unit's disbandment on 31 March 1980.

Responsibility for further Sea Harrier development was then passed over to the new Headquarters Unit, No 899 Sqn. To keep apace with FRS.Mk 1 deliveries, the Fleet Air Arm quickly stood up the frontline squadrons earmarked for carrier operations with the

As the sun slowly climbs in the east, an anonymous Sea Harrier FRS.Mk 1 sits quietly on the Yeovilton ramp awaiting the attention of the groundcrew, who will preflight the jet prior to the first sortie of the morning. The sun has picked out the rugged lines of the aircraft to good effect, the massive air intakes, and their associated blown-in doors, dominating the forward fuselage. The small vanes on the wing leading edge (called either turbulators or vortex generators) improve the airflow over the flying surfaces, each one being set at an angle to maximize its effectiveness. The twin blade aerials behind the cockpit are associated with the Decca VHF equipment, whilst the small fairing to their left is one of a pair of ram air inlets that serve the cockpit environmental control system. Within the cockpit itself, both the MDC and the all-important Smiths Industries head-up display and weapon aiming computer (HUD/WAC) are clearly visible

Sea Harrier; No 800 Sqn was recommissioned at Yeovilton on 23 April 1980, and No 801 Sqn followed suit on 28 January 1981. A third unit, No 802 Sqn, was also originally slated for reformation, but the devastating Nott defence budget of 1981 saw the newly-completed HMS *Invincible* (R05) offered to the Australian Navy, which removed the need for the ex-Sea Hawk squadron. Initially, the squadron strength of each Sea Harrier unit was restricted to five aircraft, brief cruises aboard both *Hermes* and the newly commissioned *Invincible* being performed in 1981 by Nos 800 and 801 Sqns respectively.

These initial deployments by the newly-equipped Sea Harrier squadrons were the culmination of nearly 20 years' work by firstly Hawker Siddeley and, in its later guise, British Aerospace, which had seen the diminutive P.1127 progress from an interesting novelty in the Admiralty's eyes, to their main carrier-borne weapon for the next two decades and beyond. The first carrier landing by the P.1127 had been performed with little fuss by Hawker's chief test pilot Bill Bedford aboard HMS *Ark Royal* (R09) on 8 February 1963, this particular event marking the start of a series of trials flown by Bedford, and his deputy Hugh Merewether, whilst the carrier sailed in Lyme Bay, off Portland. Although no problems were encountered over five days of flying, the Navy's response was lukewarm and the men from Hawker's returned to Kingston and pressed on with the P.1127's development for the RAF. Seven years later, with the newly delivered Harrier GR.Mk 1 just entering frontline service, the aircraft was again despatched to sea. A pair of factory-fresh Harriers from the RAF's initial development batch (which totalled six airframes) were embarked aboard HMS *Eagle* (R05) in the summer of 1970, the results obtained during this brief cruise being used to good effect the following year when a four-ship detachment from No 1 Sqn spent 12 days aboard *Ark Royal*.

The two RAF detachments, plus the initial P.1127 trials and subsequent evaluations with its Kestrel derivative, still failed to impress the Navy. However, political considerations dictated otherwise, and when the Navy lost its new generation of 50,000-ton CVA-01 carriers, they looked to the smaller 'through deck' assault vessel as a way to retain some organic fixed-wing air power. Designed primarily for the anti-submarine warfare role, these new politically-titled 'through deck cruisers' would weigh in at about 18,000 tons and be capable of carrying a mixed rotary and fixed-wind air group that numbered about 15 aircraft. No catapult or arrestor wires were to be installed in the proposed vessel, so the only aircraft that could fit the Navy's brief for its new *Invincible* class 'cruisers' was the Harrier.

Nautical GR.Mk 3

In 1971 a Naval Staff Requirement was issued to Hawker Siddeley for the development of a seagoing version of the Harrier GR.Mk 3, the Admiralty stipulating from the outset that the proposed aircraft must have a radar suitable for its air defence role, and that any magnesium in the airframe had to be replaced by non-corrosive material. To fulfil the first of these requirements, the designers at Kingston looked to Ferranti, who were at the time developing the compact ARI 5979 Sea Spray radar for eventual fitment into the new Westland Lynx HAS.Mk 2 helicopter. Following tradition, the system was quickly given a new name to differentiate this version from the primarily surface search radar on order for the Lynx. Called Blue Fox, the new radar was optimized for air-to-air search modes, functioning in I-band and utilizing frequency agility to combat systems jamming. To eliminate the corrosion problem no less that seven magnesium components were deleted from the airframe construction and two major assemblies were replaced with suitability resistant alloys in the engine.

The first order for 24 Sea Harrier FRS (Fighter, Reconnaissance, Strike).Mk 1s was placed in May 1975, these aircraft being built to a fixed-price contract. Three development batch Sea Harriers were also ordered in an effort to speed up testing and service clearance trials, these aircraft later being issued to frontline squadrons. The first Sea Harrier FRS.Mk 1 took to the skies on 20 August 1978 when chief test pilot John Farley flew XZ450 on a short sortie from Dunsfold. Built as the first of the production aircraft, this FRS.Mk 1 actually flew four months before the first of the development airframes! The hand over of completed airframes to the Navy proceeded at a relentless pace over the next four years, the initial order for 24 FRS.Mk 1s being increased to 31 (plus the three development airframes) just prior to XZ450's maiden flight. The final Sea Harrier delivery took place, rather fortuitously, just as the Royal Navy's Task Force 317 was heading south on *Operation Corporate*.

'La Muerta Negra' (The Black Death)

Having experienced less than two years of operational V/STOL flying with their new fighters, it was left to the 36 qualified Sea Harrier pilots embarked on board the *Hermes* and *Invincible* to provide the British forces in the Falklands with total air cover, a task that was to be made doubly difficult due to the fleet's glaring lack of a dedicated airborne early warning platform. When the carriers left Portsmouth on 5 April 1982 their decks were overflowing with Fleet Air Arm hardware; 20 Sea Harriers and 45 helicopters to be precise. Twelve FRS.Mk 1s of the recently strengthened No 800 Sqn lined the decks of the *Hermes*, whilst six Sea Harriers were firmly lashed to the deck of *Invincible*, a further two aircraft joining the vessel in the Channel direct from Yeovilton. As the ships sailed south so the pilots rapidly notched up the training sorties, *Hermes*, for example, maintaining a flying schedule of 40 trips a day. All Sea Harrier mission profiles were practiced, the pilots spending a considerable period of time familiarizing themselves with the new AIM-9L Sidewinders that had been hurriedly delivered to the squadrons immediately prior to sailing. This three way partnership of pilot/aircraft/missile was to prove irresistible in the South Atlantic.

The Sea Harrier's debut over the Falkland Islands was made at dawn on 1 May when all 20 aircraft were involved on strikes against Port Stanley and Goose Green airfields. Only slight damage was inflicted on one aircraft and all FRS.Mk 1s were safely recovered. The pilots, however, had little time to reflect on the success of the mission as Argentine Mirage and Dagger fighters were rapidly scrambled from their mainland bases and sent out to test the task force's defences. After eight hours of high-level sparing with these aircraft, two Sea Harriers from No 801 Sqn finally achieved a 'merge' with a pair of *Grupo* 8 Mirage IIIEAs, the French interceptors being despatched with a pair of Sidewinders (the latter Mirage had been badly damaged by one of the missiles and Argentine defensive batteries at Port Stanley airfield erroneously shot it down when it attempted to land on the island). These two Mirages were the first of 23 Argentine aircraft to be shot down by the FRS.Mk 1 in the Falklands, the final kills, three A-4B Skyhawks of *Grupo* 5, being claimed by No 800 Sqn on 8 June. No Sea Harriers were shot down by the Argentine Air Force, although two were lost to enemy groundfire and four were written off in non-combat related accidents.

Right *The preflight check is an important ritual carried out by thousands of pilots across the globe each and every day. When it comes to the ramp walkaround of a Sea Harrier, the pilot has a few extra things to check on top of the more routine flaps, ailerons and external stores. Here, Lt Dicky Payne checks that the all-important reaction control valves (RCV) are free of restrictions, and clear of any FOD. There are four RCVs fitted to the Sea Harrier; one below the radome; a single nozzle which can exhaust either up or down on each of the outrigger fairings; and the tail RCVs, which blast out in both directions laterally, as well as a third pitch control device that is vented downwards. These RCVs take the place of conventional control surfaces when the pilot transitions the aircraft from horizontal to vertical flight. As soon as the pilot positions the nozzle selector to jet-lift, high-pressure bleed air from the engine is automatically ducted to the RCVs, which vent the gases according to inputs placed on the local flying control surfaces by the pilot. This system sees the nose-down RCV in the tail controlled by a linkage from the tailplane, the horizontal yaw vents linked to the rudder, and the outrigger (roll control) devices paired with their respective port or starboard aileron. The nose-up RCV is linked directly to the pilot's control column as no traditional moveable surface exists in this area. Each blast from a fully open duct is roughly equivalent to 3000 horsepower*

Ten years on

As mentioned earlier, most of the veterans of this brief, but bloody, conflict have now moved out of the Sea Harrier community. A quick check of the Fleet Air Arm's current airframe listing reveals that of the 28 FRS.Mk 1s ultimately used in the Falklands, only nine are still currently in squadron service and two are held in storage. Of course there are more than 11 Sea Harriers in service with the fleet today, attrition replacement batches of 14 and 9 aircraft being ordered in July 1982 and September 1984 respectively. These aircraft are virtually identical to the older FRS.Mk 1s, the Sea Harrier force having received very little in the way of specification updates in its 13 years of service. The past decade has seen the two frontline units deployed on a frenetic sequence of WestLant (Western Atlantic) cruises and long deployments to the Far East and Australasia. In an effort to maintain an effective operational schedule whilst on these extended cruises, Nos 800 and 801 Sqns have increased their aircraft strength to eight FRS.Mk 1s, No 899 Sqn usually controlling roughly the same number of single-seat Sea Harriers as well.

Although the Sea Harrier can carry an assortment of freefall ordnance ranging from cluster bomb units to Mk 82 500 lb Snakeye devices, the offensive weaponry on this FRS.Mk 1 is restricted to four 25 lb 'blue' practice bombs loaded into a centreline dispenser, plus 300 rounds in the Aden gun pods. This limited assortment of ordnance will be expended on a variety of static targets scattered across the Holbeach range on the Norfolk coast, Lt Payne's Sea Harrier being one of four jets from No 800 Sqn participating in the training sortie. The sooty deposits around the blast suppression ports on the cannon pod suggest that the aircraft has already spent some time over Holbeach prior to this flight

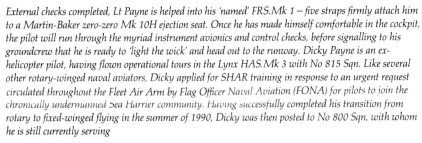

External checks completed, Lt Payne is helped into his 'named' FRS.Mk 1 – five straps firmly attach him to a Martin-Baker zero-zero Mk 10H ejection seat. Once he has made himself comfortable in the cockpit, the pilot will run through the myriad instrument avionics and control checks, before signalling to his groundcrew that he is ready to 'light the wick' and head out to the runway. Dicky Payne is an ex-helicopter pilot, having flown operational tours in the Lynx HAS.Mk 3 with No 815 Sqn. Like several other rotary-winged naval aviators, Dicky applied for SHAR training in response to an urgent request circulated throughout the Fleet Air Arm by Flag Officer Naval Aviation (FONA) for pilots to join the chronically undermanned Sea Harrier community. Having successfully completed his transition from rotary to fixed-winged flying in the summer of 1990, Dicky was then posted to No 800 Sqn, with whom he is still currently serving

The Senior Pilot (SP) at No 800 Sqn in 1990 was Lt Cdr Mel Robinson, a veteran SHAR pilot who had been flying FRS.Mk 1s since 1982. Besides having logged hundreds of hours on the Fleet Air Arm's V/STOL fighter, Lt Cdr Robinson has also completed an exchange posting with VMA-513 'Flying Nightmares', thus becoming one of the very few pilots in the Navy to have a dual rating on both the FRS.Mk 1 and the AV-8B. The Fleet Air Arm's policy of nominating an SP as the commanding officer's deputy is unique to the Navy, this position always being filled by a lieutenant commander who is invariably destined to be CO eventually. A typical Sea Harrier unit usually consists of 12 to 14 aircrew, the boss being a senior lieutenant commander whilst the majority of the pilots are lieutenants, with very occasionally a sub-lieutenant fresh from No 899 Sqn included in their ranks as well. A shortage of pilots over the past two years has often left the frontline squadrons undermanned by as many as four aircrew, and has resulted in several senior lieutenant commanders being left 'in the cockpit' far longer than originally planned, although I'm sure none of them would complain about that!

All zipped up in his 'speed jeans', and wearing his bulky survival vest, a young lieutenant from No 800 Sqn checks the starboard RCV hinge to ensure that it is moving freely before climbing aboard his SHAR and heading for Holbeach. There are fewer than 40 fully qualified Sea Harrier pilots on the Fleet Air Arm books at any one time, this small community of fighter jocks enjoying a higher skill and proficiency level than any other comparable force in the world today

At the end of the day, when it's all said and done, the SHAR pilots would have to stay in the crewroom swapping war stories if it wasn't for the small band of dedicated sailors who don their overalls and cranials and head out to the flightline to get their collective hands dirty keeping the squadrons' eight jets serviceable. This particular individual is on an exchange posting from the Imperial Japanese Navy, sorry, I mean the Maritime Self-Defense Force ...

Having completed their bombing and strafing of the Holbeach range, a pair of FRS.Mk 1s head back to base at the end of another day's flying. Leading the 'Polecat' (the squadron's call sign) formation in ZD615 is Lt Al McLaren, whilst his wingman in ZD611 is none other than Lt Dicky Payne. Lt McLaren is currently the only Royal Navy Reservist qualified to fly Sea Harriers, his nine to five job during the week seeing him at the helm of a British Caledonian TriStar. When this photograph was taken in October 1990, Lt McLaren's talents as a qualified weapons instructor (AWI) were greatly in demand by No 800 Sqn, the unit being totally devoid of an AWI at the time. Lt McLaren tries to keep his SHAR qualification valid by flying with one of the three Yeovilton-based units at least once a month

Just to prove all eight practice bombs were expended on the range, the 'Polecats' indulge in a little 'follow my leader' ahead of the FRADU Hunter T.Mk 7 photoship, flown by senior Flight Refuelling pilot Bryan Grant. The small yellow rectangles under the nose of the Sea Harriers are the flat antennae surfaces for the aircraft's Decca Doppler 72 navigation radar. This equipment is linked to the Ferranti navigation, heading and reference system (NavHARS) by an 8k-word computer to give the pilot a highly accurate grid reference reading at all times. The NavHARS allows the aircraft's navigation computer to 'level out' on a pitching carrier deck. It achieves this by utilizing a twin-gyro platform, the accuracy of which is monitored by the Doppler 72

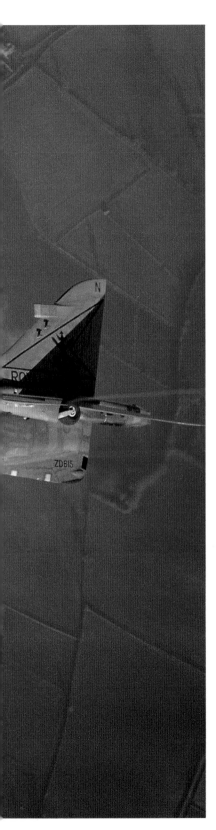

Left *Lt McLaren tucks his aircraft in tightly alongside the Hunter, the high G-induced vortices streaming off the wingtips in the moist autumn air. This particular SHAR was the last airframe built in the second production batch of 14 ordered on 1 July 1982 as both war attrition replacements and aircraft for the third airwing to be embarked aboard the* Invincible *class carrier HMS Ark Royal R07. Delivered as '005' to No 801 Sqn in January 1988, the aircraft was approaching its first major overhaul when this photograph was taken in October 1990, ZD615 being flown up to RAF St Athan for deep maintenance work and short term storage the following month. Currently still missing from Fleet Air Arm squadron listings as this book went to press, it is likely that ZD615 has been returned to British Aerospace for updating to FRS.Mk 2 specs. The current 'Polecat 124' is ZD579, this aircraft having previously served with both Nos 800 and 899 Sqns prior to its most recent tour of duty*

Above *Having cycled down the main gear and outriggers (an action which is accompanied by the automatic deployment of the the small ventral airbrake), Lt McLaren lines ZD615 up with the long runway at Yeovilton. Like its 'crab' cousin, the GR.Mk 3, the FRS.Mk 1 lands quite quickly when compared to the 'big winged' GR.Mk 5/7. Frontline units tend not to carry out too many vertical landings during a typical week's flying at Yeovilton, the FRS.Mk 1's modest fuel reserves being used to maximum effect on relatively long bombing or ACM sorties. More vertical work does appear on daily flying schedules in the weeks prior to a carrier embarkation however, as squadron pilots endeavour to reacquaint themselves with flightdeck recovery techniques on a stationary 'target' before heading out to sea*

Above *Approaching the deck of the Ark Royal from the traditional rear port quarter, Sea Harrier FRS.Mk 1 ZD614 of No 800 Sqn leads ZD582 of No 801 Sqn towards the carrier. At the time of their visit in November 1990, the Ark was also playing host to the two Sea Harrier FRS.Mk 2 prototypes which had been flown aboard for 12 days of trials work in the Channel. This aircraft carries a bomb dispenser in the traditional underfuselage position, and a single AIM-9L Sidewinder on each outer wing pylon. A twin-launcher pylon is also available for fitment to the FRS.Mk 1, this particular store being rapidly cleared for frontline use during the Falklands conflict in April 1982*

Far left *With the day's flying over, the No 800 Sqn technicians swarm over one of the unit's eight FRS.Mk 1s in an attempt to fix a minor glitch in the aircraft's armament control panel; this system ensures that the practice bombs are released when the pilot hits the 'pickle switch' on the control column. The squadron's engineering department strives to keep their jets on the ramp as much as possible, fixing as many niggling gripes as they can out in the open. Generally, the SHARs will only see the inside of the squadron hangar should a major technical fault manifest itself, Sea Harriers, like most other fast jets, tending to become more unreliable the longer they are grounded. Rarely will an engineering department head be able to report at the morning briefing that all eight aircraft are serviceable and ready for flying, six airworthy airframes tending to be the target aimed for. Even within these six aircraft there will be certain components that are temporarily U/S, although the operability of these systems will of course have been deemed not mission critical for flight safety. Generally, the Sea Harriers overall reliability has been praised by pilots and maintainers alike, estimated figures showing that for every hour the aircraft is aloft, ten man hours are spent on the ground maintaining it*

Devoid of external stores, bar the almost obligatory 190-gal droptanks, ZD582 is positioned over the deck by the No 801 Sqn boss, Lt Cdr Mike 'Soapy' Watson. An Operation Corporate veteran, Lt Cdr Watson was one of the select band of senior pilots retained in flying postings during the aircrew shortage crisis of 1990/91. Having completed a two-year stint in command of No 800 Sqn at the end of 1989, 'Soapy' was then posted to a desk job within the FONA organization. However, the need for an experienced 'SHAR driver' at the helm of No 801 Sqn saw an urgent call go out for Lt Cdr Watson, who duly took command of the unit from Lt Cdr J A Siebert on 20 March 1990. One of the last combat veterans still flying within the SHAR community today, Lt Cdr Watson was actually still undergoing his conversion onto the type with No 899 Sqn in April 1982 when he was despatched (along with three other students and four instructors) firstly to Hermes but then finally across to Invincible and No 801 Sqn. Described by legendary Sea Harrier pilot Lt Cdr Nigel 'Sharkey' Ward (then CO of No 801 Sqn) as a 'most professional operator', Watson flew with extreme skill throughout the campaign. Upon his return to the UK he served with No 801 Sqn again, before returning to No 899 Sqn in 1984 as an instructor

In April 1990 Ark Royal, and her associated battle group, sailed out of the Mediterranean and headed west across the mid-Atlantic, bound for New York. Over the following four months, the carrier cruised up and down the eastern seaboard exercising with elements of both the US Navy and the Canadian Armed Forces as part of the Royal Navy's annual WestLant deployment. During that time, the eight embarked Sea Harrier FRS.Mk 1s of No 801 Sqn also enjoyed some fraternization with the air arms of both nations, the unit spending three weeks, for example, shorebased at Naval Air Station (NAS) Cecil Field in Florida, whilst the Ark was docked at nearby NAS Mayport. Of the eight SHARs assigned to No 801 Sqn, this anonymous example was the youngest airframe embarked, ZE698 in fact being the last FRS.Mk 1 delivered to the Fleet Air Arm on 16 August 1988. The final Sea Harrier of batch three, this aircraft, along with six others in the nine-strong order, was flown from Dunsfold to St Athan for storage, pending its conversion to FRS.Mk 2 specs. However, a shortage of FRS.Mk 1s in frontline service saw both ZE698 and sister airframe ZE693 issued to No 801 Sqn straight from storage in February/March 1990. A close look at this aircraft reveals just how new it was in April 1990, the Yeovilton paint shop having not even had the time to adorn the jet's fin with the traditional No 801 Sqn trident and chequered rudder before the Sea Harrier was flown out to Ark Royal. Two years later, as this book went to press, ZE698 was still with the squadron, although it now wears side number '004'

Above *By wearing a red coat with a vertical black stripe you become responsible for anything offensive that may find its way under the wing of a Sea Harrier. Braving high winds and squally showers, the small band of highly skilled armourers from No 801 Sqn systematically bomb up four of the unit's SHARs with a variety of weapons for a live firing exercise during WestLant '90. This particular weapon is a bog-standard 1000 lb Mk 13 HE bomb, five of which could be carried on a very short mission by the SHAR. A more typical configuration, however, would see two or three of these devices spread between the outer pylons and the centreline stores station. The armourers have to ensure that the linkages between the ordnance and the pylon are secured properly because a hung up bomb will place the SHAR's centre of gravity out of limits when it comes to a vertical recovery back aboard ship, forcing the pilot to eject if he cannot reach landfall*

Above left *Whilst the Ark replenishes her stocks of diesel oil and Avtur from the Royal Fleet Auxiliary ship Olna, the deckcrew of No 801 Sqn takes advantage of this lull in the flying programme to ready the Sea Harriers for the next launch. Sitting proudly atop ZE693 in his brown surcoat (which denotes that he is an engine and airframe technician), this naval airman is topping up the aircraft's demineralised injection system tank with distillate. The traditional naval practice of allocating the ramp area of the carrier deck to the embarked fighter squadron is perpetrated by both SHAR units during their periods at sea*

Far left *With his jet safely back aboard the carrier, the pilot has vacated his SHAR and headed back down below decks for a debrief in the squadron ready room, leaving the aircraft handlers (blue coats) to marshal the FRS.Mk 1 back to its allocated parking spot on the stern of the ship. Operating the aircraft's brakes is a green-coated sailor from the electrical trade, the Ninja Turtle motif on his cranial being clearly visible through the canopy transparency. The Sea Harrier cockpit is positioned 11 in higher than the GR.Mk 3's, this modification providing the British Aerospace engineers with more equipment space beneath the floor. These alterations also saw the general cockpit layout drastically changed, and the whole 'front office' covered with a true fighter-style bubble canopy*

Above *Arguably the most famous Sea Harrier ever built, XZ457 came back from the Falklands aboard the* Hermes *wearing three white kill silhouettes beneath the cockpit, the aircraft actually being responsible for the shooting down of four Argentine aircraft. One of 12 FRS.Mk 1s assigned to No 800 Sqn, XZ457 went to war as 'black 14', being flown on numerous bombing and CAP sorties during the campaign. The aircraft's first kills came on the afternoon of 21 May 1982 following the amphibious landing at San Carlos that morning. Flying a CAP at 10,000 ft over Goose Green, Lt Clive 'Spag' Morell in XZ457 and Flt Lt John Leeming in XZ500 responded to urgent calls for help from the Type 21 frigate HMS Ardent, which was under attack from three A-4Q Skyhawks of the Argentine Navy's 3rd Naval fighter and Attack Escuadrilla. Swooping down after the fleeing jets, Morell quickly achieved a missile lock on the lead A-4Q piloted by Lt Cdr Alberto Philippi. Morell seized his opportunity and loosed off a Sidewinder, the missile detonating behind the aircraft's jetpipe. With his Skyhawk pitched out of control, Philippi successfully ejected, coming down in San Carlos water just near the shoreline. Lining up on the second A-4Q in the formation (piloted by a Lt José Arca), Morell again achieved missile lock but the AIM-9L refused to fire. Quickly switching to guns, he emptied both magazines into the aircraft but could not confirm any damage. Eventually the missile did fire but it ran out of thrust before it hit the target. Badly damaged by cannon fire from both Morell's Adens and guns aboard the now sinking Ardent, the A-4Q was guided by Arca towards Port Stanley airfield, where he lined up for a landing only to find his undercarriage inoperable. Unable to set the aircraft down safely he ejected. The third Skyhawk in the formation had, in the meantime, been downed by Flt Lt Leeming with his Aden cannon. The aircraft's final kills occurred three days later when XZ457 was being flown by No 800 Sqn's boss, Lt Cdr Andy Auld; his wingman on this occasion was Lt Dave Smith in ZA193 (this aircraft was also embarked on Ark during WestLant '90). Vectored onto four Argentine Air Force Daggers from Grupo 6 by the Type 22 frigate HMS Broadsword, the Sea Harriers intercepted the fighters at extremely low level, Auld quickly loosing off both his Sidewinders which duly despatched two aircraft. Lt Smith followed his leader's example by locking up a third Dagger soon after the first two had gone down, splashing the jet with yet another Sidewinder. Prior to Operation Corporate, XZ457 had initially been delivered to No 700A Sqn from Dunsfold in January 1980, the aircraft then going to No 899 Sqn in August when the IFTU was disbanded. Still with the training unit when the taskforce was put together in April 1982, the aircraft's brief but colourful association with No 800 Sqn ended with the cessation of hostilities and the SHARs triumphant return to Yeovilton. Re-acquainted with the 'Polecats' in April 1988 following a major overhaul, XZ457 eventually found its way to No 801 Sqn in March 1990, fresh from a short spell in the Aircraft Maintenance Group's hangar at Yeovilton*

Right *Fellow Falklands veteran ZA193 sits quietly on the stern of Ark, resting between sorties. Freshly delivered to No 800 Sqn from St Athan immediately prior to the unit's embarkation aboard the* Hermes *in early April 1982, this aircraft went on to serve with the short-lived No 809 Sqn post-Operation Corporate, before being reissued to No 801 Sqn in January 1983. Linked with this unit ever since, ZA193 has just returned to frontline service following a lengthy period in overhaul at St Athan*

Above *The brightly jacketed deckcrew lean into the turn as Ark heels over in search of a decent headwind. Ready for launch, Lt Cdr 'Soapy' Watson sits patiently in his jet, ZD609 already ticking over. Once the ship has finished its radical manoeuvring, the nose leg shackles and the wheel chock will be removed and Watson will take his foot off the brakes and blip the throttle, moving the SHAR forward to the launch spot. Wearing the traditional '000' codes which distinguish the CO's mount in No 801 Sqn, ZD609 completed the cruise and was then sent to St Athan for overhaul, returning to the unit as '006' in December 1990. On 10 May 1991, whilst undertaking a simulated low-level strike on the Severn Bridge from his Yeovilton base, the pilot of ZD609 experienced severe problems with his jet, and unable to regain height he was forced to eject at extremely low level, ZD609 crashing and burning out in woodland near the Welsh town of Chepstow*

Right *Steaming into the breeze, Ark prepares to launch one of its SHARs off the bow ski jump. Controlling the Sea Harrier at deck level is a yellow-jacketed Flightdeck Officer (FDO); usually a high-time petty officer, the FDO is greatly respected by both pilots and deck crew alike. Only a privileged few get to wear an FDO surcoat and wave the small green flag. When the wind speed over the ramp is correct and the pilot has signalled that everything is operable in the cockpit, the FDO will quickly glance up at FlyCo (Flight Control, which is situated on the port side of the bridge) and when he sees the 'traffic light' arrangement go to fixed green, he will rapidly bring his flag down in a windmilling motion. The pilot will release the brakes and the Sea Harrier will power down the deck. Removed from the harsh noise and stiff wind up in FlyCo are the Flying Control Officer (normally a Lt Cdr), known as 'Little F', and his boss, Commander (Air), who is universally known throughout the ship as 'Wings'. These two officers are responsible for flight safety on the ship whilst the vessel is at flying stations*

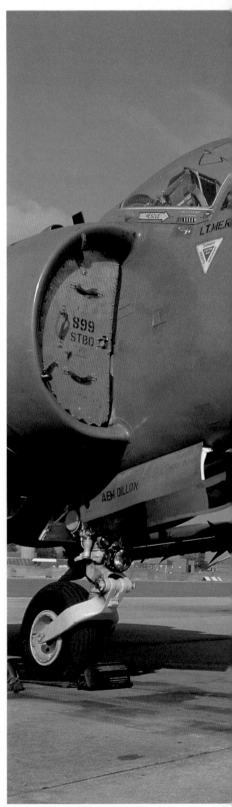

Above *Mission accomplished, the SHARs approach and land aboard the Ark from the carrier's port rear quarter. A typical four-ship formation will recover aboard the vessel in under two minutes, the pilots slowly taxying towards the bow of the carrier to make room for the next aircraft. Once all the jets are down, the pilots can either shut the power off and let the deck handlers push the Sea Harriers back to the stern area using the carriers tow tractors, or they can keep the engines running and reverse taxy (under the supervision of the blue jackets) into their allotted spots*

Right *Although operating the largest force of Sea Harriers in the Fleet Air Arm, the 'winged-fisted' No 899 Sqn have not seen a carrier deck since March 1984. Tasked with training fledgling naval aviators in the art of V/STOL flying, Royal Navy style, the squadron usually operates eight to ten FRS.Mk 1s, plus a mixed bag of four or five two-seat T.Mk 4 Harriers and two Blue Fox-equipped Hunter T.Mk 8Ms. Having completed their basic flying training with the RAF on Tucanos and Hawks, pilots then accrue stick time on the No 899 Sqn fleet over a six- to eight-month period. The recommended flight time on the various aircraft in the squadron is as follows; 28 hours on the Harrier T.Mk 4A; eight hours and ten minutes on the Hunter T.Mk 8M for Blue Fox radar familiarization; 11 hours and 15 minutes on the Harrier T.Mk 4N; and 72 hours ten minutes on the Sea Harrier*

Above *A suitably patriotic naval airman checks the hinges on one of the eight blow-in doors built into the FRS.Mk 1's engine intakes. As well as providing pilots for fleet units, No 899 Sqn also trains both officers and ratings in various supporting fields for eventual frontline postings*

Left *Taxying into the early morning sun, this anonymous jet was one of a pair of FRS.Mk 1s flown across to RAF Wittering in September 1990 for inclusion in the GR.Mk 5 formation put up as part of the Battle of Britain flypast. Flown by instructor pilots, the Sea Harriers spent most of the week prior to 15 September participating in rehearsal flights from the Cambridgeshire base. Up until 1 January 1989, all ab initio Sea Harrier training had been carried out at Wittering by No 233 OCU, this task then being passed over to No 899 Sqn, along with several ex-RAF T.Mk 4A two-seat Harriers. As can be clearly seen on this aircraft, the squadron's FRS.Mk 1s rarely carry Aden cannon pods beneath the fuselage, two small cushion augmentation strakes usually being fitted in their place*

Above *For the first four years of its existence, No 899 Sqn had no two-seat Harriers at all, the unit carrying out all its conversion training on FRS.Mk 1s and a pair of blue Fox-equipped Hunters. The first T.Mk 4 ordered by the Fleet Air Arm (XZ445) was delivered directly to the RAF in June 1979 as an aid for ab initio pilot training, then carried out by the OCU. Eventually transferred to Yeovilton in January 1988, XZ445 joined two T.Mk 4Ns that had been in service at the air station since 1980. These aircraft were the survivors of a batch of three ordered by the Navy in 1981. Designated T.Mk 4Ns primarily because they lack the LRMTS laser nose as fitted in the T.Mk 4A, these aircraft also have a more FRS.Mk 1 orientated instrument layout in the twin cockpits. Maintained in pristine condition, this T.Mk 4N (ZB605) was decorated with a low-viz shark's mouth in 1990*

Right *Just under 12 months later, with its 'gnashers' removed, ZB605 is carefully pulled apart by several of the unit's female ratings. With the rear canopy fairing removed, the internal ducting for the all-important cockpit airconditioning system is exposed to the elements. Unlike the single-seat FRS.Mk 1, the T.Mk 4s are 'tin nosed', the slender confines of the aircrafts' radome being too small to hold a Blue Fox radar – hence the need for the modified Hunter T.Mk 8Ms*

Ark and the 'Mk 2

An important milestone in the Sea Harrier FRS.Mk 2 programme was passed in November 1990 when the two pre-production aircraft deployed from British Aerospace Dunsfold to the *Ark Royal* for ten days of exhaustive sea trials. Supported by 28 British Aerospace personnel and 8 observers from A & AEE Boscombe Down, the two aircraft were jointly flown by two company and two service pilots.

Whilst embarked aboard the *Ark*, the FRS.Mk 2s launched and recovered with a number of different weapons fitments including AIM-120 AMRAAMs, twin AIM-9L Sidewinder rails and 1000 lb HE bombs. Overall, a total of 40 plus sorties were flown between the two aircraft.

One FRS.Mk 2 (XV439) was fully kitted out with an operational Ferranti Blue Vixen radar, although the standard of software fitted was not as advanced as that carried in British Aerospace's trials BAe 125; the second airframe (ZA195) carried no radar at all. Coincidentally, XV439 had also experienced extensive trialling in its earlier form as an FRS.Mk 1, this particular airframe being the middle aircraft of three development batch machines utilized by British Aerospace during the Sea Harrier programme in 1978/79.

The main purpose of the sea trial period was to prove the FRS.Mk 2's compatibility with the *Invincible* class carriers, both in terms of launch and recovery performance and avionics suitability. Chief Sea Harrier FRS.Mk 2 project pilot, Rod Fredericksen, described the British Aerospace brief for the aircrafts' time at sea as basically a chance to prove that the data gleaned ashore was correct in an operational environment, rather than an attempt to push back any frontiers.

'What we need to show to MoD (PE) is that the aircraft is basically an FRS.Mk 1 in terms of its deck handling and launch performance, and that the predictions for the FRS.Mk 2 configurations work as advertised at sea. I think its launch characteristics are the main crux of this trial, some avionics data also being accrued along the way'.

One modification tested ashore that wasn't trialled aboard the *Ark* was the extra span wingtips originally designed for use with the FRS.Mk 2 when the aircraft was carrying AMRAAMs. Theoretically, the bolt-on tips (which increased the FRS.Mk 2's wing span

The shape of things to come – Sea Harrier FRS.Mk 2 XZ439 edges closer to Ark Royal's flightdeck prior to landing aboard for the very first time. One of the two FRS.Mk 1s modified by British Aerospace for development trials with the new systems planned for the entire Sea Harrier fleet, this redesignated Mk 2 completed its first flight fitted with a B-model Blue Vixen radar on 24 May 1990. One of three pre-production Sea Harrier FRS.Mk 1s built for the Fleet Air Arm, this aircraft has spent most of its life with either the Aerospace and Armament Experimental Establishment (A & AEE) at Boscombe Down, or with British Aerospace. Initially issued to A Sqn A & AEE in April 1982, along with fellow pre-production airframes XZ338 and XZ440, this aircraft performed the vital AIM-9L Sidewinder compatibility trials at RAF Valley that same month, passing the twin-missile rail pylon for service use soon after. Called up temporarily for frontline duty to fill the gaps created in the training fleet by the issue of Yeovilton-based SHARs to fleet units, XZ439 carried out deck trials aboard the newly commissioned HMS Illustrious (R06) whilst wearing the 'winged fist' of No 899 Sqn on its tail in July 1982. Returned to British Aerospace two months later, the aircraft has remained with them ever since

Above *XZ439's pilot on the historic flight out from Dunsfold to the carrier in November 1990 was Lt Cdr Simon Hargreaves, the Fleet Air Arm's senior pilot with the A & AEE at the time. It was as a young lieutenant fresh from conversion training, and recently posted to No 800 Sqn, that Hargreaves made history on 21 April 1982 when he intercepted the first Argentine military aircraft of Operation Corporate. Performing an operational patrol armed with two live AIM-9Ls and 300 rounds of 30 mm ammunition, Hargreaves made contact with an Argentine Air Force Boeing 707–320B that was shadowing the battle group 150 nautical miles south of the carrier Invincible. Under strict orders not to fire at the aircraft, he proceeded to guide the 707 away from the fleet instead. Eight years later, and aboard a different carrier, Hargreaves signals to the tractor driver that he has reapplied the brakes. The white sphere tucked down the side of the instrument coaming is not a new antenna dish; it is in fact Hargreaves' cap!*

Right *The second FRS.Mk 2 embarked for the ten-day trial period in early November 1990 was ZA195, the original prototype Mk 2 constructed by British Aerospace. Flown for the first time in this configuration on 19 September 1988, the aircraft has served primarily as an aerodynamic testbed devoid of the Blue Vixen radar, and its associated equipment. Embodying all the physical changes destined for the Mk 2 like the jumboised radome, lengthened (by 1 ft) rear fuselage and kinked leading edge, ZA195 was flown aboard the Ark by British Aerospace's Chief Sea Harrier FRS.Mk 2 project pilot, Rod Fredericksen. The last FRS.Mk 1 of the first production batch of 31 aircraft, ZA195 served briefly with No 899 Sqn in late 1984 before being passed back to British Aerospace for FRS.Mk 2 trials work*

by 2 ft) gave the Sea Harrier increased manoeuvre stability in any weapons configuration. However, the excellent handling qualities of the tried and tested British Aerospace design negated the need for them, as Rod Fredericksen explained.

'There was a design requirement to meet a certain spec regarding the aircraft's inflight characteristics, but that has since been relaxed a little because the handling qualities of the FRS.Mk 2 are so good. Although this decision is not 100 per cent firm, we are not trialling them on this embarkation, a factor which speaks for itself I think.'

The tips have been flown in stability trials which have centred around a new underwing tank that the Navy initially requested. It was predicted that the stability figure stipulated for the FRS.Mk 2 with these new tanks, and an AMRAAM round under each wing, could only be reached with the tips in place. However, the Navy has since decided to retain the present 190 Imp gal (864 litre) two compartment tanks so long associated with the FRS.Mk 1.

'The final say on the configuration still depends on the Royal Navy's drop tank requirement. If they continue to use the present tanks then no problems arise. However, if they go for a three-compartment tank then the tips may still come into play. Negotiations have taken place between British Aerospace and the MoD and hopefully a common ground has been found which will suit everyone concerned. The aircraft is certainly sound without the tips fitted. MoD is happy with that, Boscombe Down are satisfied and so are we', Rod Fredericksen stated affirmatively.

Since the sea trials, work has continued apace on developing the aircraft's Blue Vixen radar, GEC-Ferranti and British Aerospace working extensively with both airframes. ZA195 is currently with the A & AEE at Boscombe Down undergoing testing that will see its radar pitted against multiple targets that have a jamming capability, Blue Vixen's interface with the FRS.Mk 2's weapons systems being particularly scrutinized. These trials are expected to last two years.

Joining ZA195 at Boscombe Down very shortly will be XZ497, the first reworked production standard Mk 2. This aircraft will eventually be issued to the Operational Evaluation Unit (OEU) after it has completed cold hangar and general environmental control tests. The OEU will in time move to Yeovilton when there are sufficient FRS.Mk 2s available to re-equip No 899 Sqn. Prior to this milestone event, the aircraft must first complete its hot weather trials and the vital AMRAAM firing tests at Eglin AFB in Florida.

Looking suitably pleased with himself after completing the first landing of an FRS.Mk 2 aboard a Royal Navy carrier, Rod Fredericksen admires the view from his Martin-Baker ejection seat as a slightly embarrassed deck crew from British Aerospace scramble around below him looking for a ladder to attach to the aircraft's side! No stranger to a carrier deck, Fredericksen is a retired lieutenant commander with over 2000 hours on FRS.Mk 1s in his logbook; he was in fact only the second naval aviator ever to fly the Sea Harrier. Mentioned in Despatches during his time with No 800 Sqn in the Falklands, Fredericksen was credited with both a Dagger and an Argentine naval patrol boat in the conflict. Given command of No 800 Sqn in the mid-1980s, Fredericksen left the Navy in late 1988, bound for British Aerospace and the FRS.Mk 2 programme. Sharing the flying duties with him during the ten-day trial aboard the Ark were British Aerospace Dunfold's deputy chief test pilot, Graham Tomlinson (ex-GR.Mk 3s) and the A & AEE's Flt Lt David Mackay (GR.Mk 3s and Mk 5s)

The most obvious difference between the old Mk 1 and the revised Mk 2 is the enlarged radome, its bulbous appearance resulting from the Blue Vixen's larger diameter radar scanner, and the increased 'black boxes' that go to make up the system itself. The choice of the multi-mode pulse doppler radar for the Mk 2 was basically dictated by the Royal Navy's requirement for the aircraft to be fitted with the Hughes AIM-120 Advanced Medium-Range Air-to-Air Missile (AMRAAM). The Blue Vixen is capable of tracking targets at long-range over both land and sea, its look down/shoot down capability far exceeding that currently on offer from the austere Blue Fox. In total, the Blue Vixen has no less than 11 modes covering air-to-air and air-to-surface operations. In the former category the aircraft can look up, look down, velocity search, air combat, track-while-scan and single target track. Its air-to-surface capabilities include real beam ground mapping, sea surface search, beacon interrogation, ranging and freezing data. From this low angle the twin pitot heads, which replace the dominant nose mounted 'spear' on the Mk 1, are clearly visible below the radome of XZ439

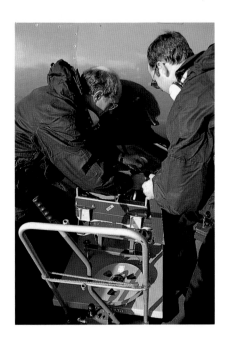

Above *Two civilian engineers gently up load a hard-tape recording device into the aft equipment bay of ZA195. This complex piece of kit recorded all the control inputs placed on the aircraft's flying surfaces by the pilot, each reel being replaced after every sortie, and the information encoded on the tape deciphered below decks in the comfort of a former squadron ready-room, taken over by British Aerospace technicians during the brief cruise*

Right *Wearing special calibration chequers on its nose and tail, ZA195 has its injection tank replenished prior to a dusk sortie flown by Flt Lt Dave Mackay to test the aircraft's MADGE (Microwave Aircraft Digital Guidance Equipment), and its interface with information fed to it from the ship. Prior to this deployment, Flt Lt Mackay had never operated from a flightdeck in his service career, although by the end of the trial he had flown roughly a quarter of the 40 plus trips generated during the cruise*

Left *Landing lights ablaze, Flt Lt Mackay gently descends towards the ramp having completed the short MADGE sortie. The FRS.Mk 2 should enter squadron service at the end of 1992 if the development programme continues to plan, No 899 Sqn being slated as the first recipient of the new fighter. Ten brand new FRS.Mk 2s will be built by British Aerospace in a £100 million plus contract awarded in March 1990, a further 31 FRS.Mk 1s being allocated for the upgrading programme that is to run concurrently with the new-build production line. 'The time the initial return to works aeroplanes spend with British Aerospace will depend a lot on the state that they are offered up to the company in the first place. The early production airframes will obviously need more time in rework than the later ones. What you will get is a gradual decrease in the time taken to turn around FRS.Mk 1s as the level of experience increases with each upgrading to FRS.Mk 2 specs', explained Lt Cdr Fredericksen during the trials*

Above right *The AMRAAM fitment to the Mk 2 will give the Fleet Air Arm's fighter squadrons a chance to knock down enemy aircraft at beyond visual range, thus avoiding the need for a SHAR pilot to engage in the risky business of dogfighting – currently the FRS.Mk 1's primary form of attack. Toting four dummy rounds under the wings and fuselage, ZA193 launches off into the murk. The centreline rounds are fitted to US-standard LAU-106 rails developed especially for the AMRAAM, whilst the wing-mounted weapons are slung under British-built Frazer-Nash Common Rail Launchers, suitable for both AIM-9 and AIM-120 carriage. Initially, the large size of the AMRAAM and its 'flying' characteristics worried British Aerospace, wind tunnel testing showing that the missiles could cause the aircraft's aerodynamic centre of balance to shift. However, thorough testing, and the placement of the rounds congruent with the aircraft's centre of gravity, have eradicated any problems, the Mk 2s passing every launch, recovery and stability test thrust upon them whilst at sea*

Right *The radar-equipped XZ439 powers away from the Ark at the start of yet another proving flight. Each launch was videotaped by technicians aboard the ship, the aircrafts' weight also being carefully annotated and its take-off roll commencement point moved up and down the flightdeck*

Exports

Aside from the US Marine Corps, the service with the longest record of Harrier operations at sea is the *Arma Aérea de la Armada*, or the Spanish Naval Air Arm. Boasting a small, but highly experienced cadre of naval aviators, the *Armada* splits its mixed Harrier force into two operational units; *Octava Escuadrilla* (*Eslla* 008) and *Novena Escuadrilla* (*Eslla* 009). Both units are based at the large facility at Rota, near Cadiz, and although they often share deck space aboard the sole Spanish carrier *Principe de Asturias* (R11), the *escuadrilla* operate vastly different model Harriers. Formed on 4 September 1976, *Eslla* 008 is equipped with the surviving AV-8A(s) and TAV-8A(s) models delivered in two batches in the late 1970s, whilst *Eslla* 009 was activated on 29 September 1987 to coincide with the delivery of 12 new EAV-8Bs built for the *Armada* at St Louis.

Fifteen years earlier, Spain had experienced its first taste of V/STOL operations when Hawker Siddeley's chief test pilot John Farley conducted two days of carrier-borne trials aboard the *Principe de Asturias'* venèrable predecessor, *Dedalo* (R01), in October 1972. Flown directly from Dunsfold to the carrier, which was sailing off the coast of Barcelona, the Harrier's brief stay aboard ship impressed the Spanish Navy so much that they ordered six single-seat and two twin-seat AV-8s less than a year later. Although these aircraft (like all other AV-8As) were built at Kingston expressly for the Spanish, they had to first be ordered and then delivered to the USMC to avoid the arms embargo that the British government was trying to enforce against General Franco's regime at the time. Following the successful introduction of these aircraft, a second batch of five AV-8A(s)s were ordered by the *Armada*, although by this stage Franco had died and the embargo had been lifted. As a result all five airframes were flown directly from Dunsfold to Rota in 1980/81. The Spanish Harriers are equipped with essentially the same systems as the Marine Corps' now retired AV-8As, although the aircrafts' radio fit was slightly modified to achieve commonality with equipment already in *Armada* service.

Indian Navy

Mysteriously, the Harrier has never been a great export success for either British Aerospace or McDonnell Douglas. The aircraft has been demonstrated to many potential operators across the globe but few of these armed forces have backed their

Operating some of the oldest Harriers still flying, Escuadrilla 008 do however, enjoy one of the newest aircraft carriers sailing the world's oceans as their at-sea base. Spending anything up to 20 days a month embarked aboard the 16,700-ton Principe de Asturias *(R11) cruising in the Mediterranean or mid-Atlantic, Escuadrilla 008 is one of the most experienced Harrier squadrons currently in existence. Wearing the serial number 01-805 on its intake, this AV-8A(S) was one of the original batch of six aircraft ordered through McDonnell Douglas from British Aerospace in 1973. Built as BuNo 159561, the aircraft was delivered with the same Baseline nav/attack system fitted to the USMC AV-8s. Approaching the* Principe de Asturias *following a successful sortie during* Display Determination '90, *the aircraft is carrying two empty five-in Zuni rocket pods, the pilot having expended all eight projectiles in the course of the mission (Duncan Cubitt/Airforces Monthly)*

enthusiastic words with firm orders. One country that was convinced by the British Aerospace product however, was India, who approached the company in early 1972. Perhaps the selling of the Sea Harrier to the Directorate of Naval Aviation should not have come as such a surprise when one considers that the Indian Navy purchased these aircraft to replace another venerable Hawker's product, the Sea Hawk. This factor, allied with the minimal deck space available aboard the Navy's sole carrier, INS *Vikrant*, virtually dictated that the Indians buy British, and they did.

Although the Spanish received their Harriers first, India actually evaluated the aircraft three months prior to the *Dedalo* visit when John Farley flew Hawker Siddeley's Harrier Mk. 52 G-VTOL across to Cochin in July 1972. Following a brief period of familiarization training for shore-based officers at the main Indian naval facility, the aircraft was embarked aboard the *Vikrant* for two days of intensive carrier operations. G-VTOL's twin-stick capabilities were used to their fullest during the tour, several senior Indian Navy pilots, including the vessel's commander air and the CO of the resident Sea Hawk squadron being checked out in the back seat of the aircraft. Their comments were all duly noted and, after further deliberation and budget juggling, the first export order for six Sea Harriers was eventually placed by the Indian government in 1980.

All pilot training on the Indian Sea Harriers (the single seaters being designated FRS.Mk 51s and the two-seaters T.Mk 60s) was initially carried out by No 233 OCU at Wittering, the pilots then moving on to the Indian Navy Training Unit, which was

Sharing deck space aboard the Principe de
Asturias *with Escuadrilla 008 during the exercise
was sister-unit Escuadrilla 009, and five of their
recently delivered EAV-8Bs. Formed at Rota on
29 September 1987, the unit operates all 11
surviving Harrier IIs of the 12 ordered from St
Louis in March 1983. The aircraft are kitted out
with the same systems fitted in the USMC AV-
8Bs, and the Spanish have benefitted greatly from
this commonality by having all their pilot
conversion training undertaken at Cherry Point
by VMAT-203. This particular aircraft is being
positioned onto the carrier's lift following a brief
stay in the hangar deck undergoing routine
maintenance*
(Duncan Cubitt/Airforces Monthly)

Principle de Asturias cruises through the gentle swells of the Mediterranean, its crew enjoying a brief respite from flying stations during the hectic three-week long exercise. Parked alongside the closest EAV-8B is an Augusta-Bell AB-212 helicopter of Escuadrilla 007. The island superstructure of the Spanish carrier is appreciably smaller than that built onto the deck of the Invincible class vessels, thus allowing more space for the embarked air wing (Duncan Cubitt/Airforces Monthly)

established at Yeovilton in December 1982. Charged with the responsibility of instructing both pilots and groundcrews alike, the unit was equipped with all six FRS.Mk 51s on order, plus a single T.Mk 60, and was parented during its time at the base by No 899 Sqn. In December 1983 a trio of FRS.Mk 51s were despatched to their new base at Goa, in southern India, the Sea Harriers being immediately issued to the Navy's premier unit, No 300 'White Tigers' Sqn, upon their arrival. The remaining aircraft remained at Yeovilton until June 1984. The squadron undertook its first full-scale deployment aboard *Vikrant* in early 1985, the Indians being so impressed with the aircrafts' performance and reliability that they ordered a second batch of 10 FRS.Mk 51s and a single T.Mk 60 in November of that year. Just under a year later a third and final request for seven single seaters and a solitary 'twin-sticker' was received by British Aerospace.

Although the Indian Navy operates only 10 few Sea Harriers than the Fleet Air Arm, and has at its disposal two carriers (*Vikrant* and the *Viraat*), No 300 Sqn is still the sole frontline operator of the FRS.Mk 51. All pilot training for the 'White Tigers' is carried out by the Sea Harrier Operational Training Unit (SHOFTU), nominally designated 'B' Flight and controlled by No 551 Sqn, which is also based at Indian Naval Station *Hansa* (Goa). The three surviving T.Mk 60s are on SHOFTU's books, as are several FRS.Mk 51s, although all three aircraft wear No 300 Sqn's 'White Tiger' emblem on their fins. To date, Sea Harrier operations in this region have remained largely unreported. Nevertheless, the potential of two modernized carriers equipped with upwards of 20 FRS.Mk 51s sailing in the Indian Ocean has not gone unnoticed by India's neighbours, this large nation now clearly possessing a truly mobile force for sustained power projection at sea.

Powered up and positioned on the flightdeck's black launch line up marker, a pair of storeless Harrier IIs prepare to roll. During the exercise, the carrier's EAV-8Bs provided CAP support for the 23 vessels of 'Green Force', which opposed the 16 warships grouped around the US Navy carrier USS Saratoga *(CV-60) that comprised 'Brown Force'* (Duncan Cubitt/Airforces Monthly)

Above *Although the Spaniards are planning to obtain two TAV-8Bs for pilot training, the only 'twin-stickers' currently in service are the original pair of TAV-8A(S)s delivered in 1976. Operated by Escuadrilla 008, the TAV-8s are used for training pilots destined for AV-8A(S)s only, the USMC no longer offering a wings course on this type following the retirement of its last TAV-8As in early 1987. Escuadrilla 008 pilots double as both frontline aircrew and instructor, this dual role placing quite a strain on the unit's eight qualified 'AV-8tors'. With the AV-8A(S) not due for retirement until the advent of the EAV-8B Plus in 1995, the requirement for suitably qualified pilots (usually three or four a year) is unlikely to decrease for some time yet. This TAV-8A(S) was the second of the two-seaters delivered, and was photographed at RAFG Gutersloh during an exchange with No IV Sqn in September 1988* (Howard Jones)

Left *Nozzles angled down and landing light ablaze, a suitably drab Harrier II touches down on the stern of the carrier. The small fillet just below the Spanish roundel is exhausting excess steam out of the 'cold' nozzle. The EAV-8Bs wear a two-tone grey scheme overall, the demarcation line between the lighter and darker shades being visible just near the pitot tube on the starboard side of the aircraft's nose* (Duncan Cubitt/Airforces Monthly)

Cruising at height over a typically thick English cloud bank, a pair of Indian Navy Sea Harrier FRS.Mk 51s indulge in a spot of formation flying for the camera. Both aircraft wear the standard extra dark sea grey and white colour scheme as originally worn on Fleet Air Arm FRS.Mk 1s, but here adorned with the Indian national roundel and the leaping white tiger emblem of No 300 Sqn. The aircraft closest to the camera is carrying two small 100-gal external tanks (the Fleet Air Arm has used the 190-gal size for some years now) and wears the code '605' on its intake. This jet was one of three Mk 51s flown out to India, via Luqa, Luxor and Dubai, on 13 December 1983, there arrival over Goa three days later signalling a new era in Indian naval aviation history. Behind IN605 is IN602, which has no three-number code on the intake and is devoid of external store, although it does carry all four wing pylons. Whilst IN605 was carrying out the first Mk 51 deck trials aboard the Vikrant *in January 1984, IN602 was being used as an instructional airframe by the Indian Navy Flying Training Unit at Yeovilton during the second Sea Harrier conversion course (British Aerospace)*

The first airframe in the third batch of seven FRS.Mk 51s ordered by the Indians in October 1986 is put through its paces whilst carrying a pair of oversize external tanks used purely for long-range ferrying purposes. The later batch Mk 51s incorporated several updates and modifications tried and operationally tested on Fleet Air Arms FRS. Mk 1s, with IN623 being the last new-build FRS.Mk 1/Mk 51 constructed by British Aerospace. The Indians have received a total of 23 single- and 4 two-seat Sear Harriers (Geoff Lee/British Aerospace)

The small band of test pilots at Dunsfold are required to carry out exhaustive pre-acceptance checks on the fighters prior to there departure for India. As many as 25 flights are made to ensure that all systems are working as advertised. Once the Indian Navy's representatives in London are satisfied, the civilian pilots then head out on the 5000-mile trek to INS Hansa, where all the Sea Harriers are shore-based with No 300 'White Tiger' Sqn (Geoff Lee/British Aerospace)